C000109357

MEXICAN

AUTHENTIC RECIPES FROM SOUTH OF THE BORDER

CONTENTS

DRINKS
SNACKS AND
STARTERS

WE USED COINTREAU FOR THIS RECIPE.
YOU CAN BUY SUGAR SYRUP FROM MOST
SUPERMARKETS OR MAKE YOUR OWN. STIR 1
CUP CASTER SUGAR WITH 1 CUP WATER IN SMALL
SAUCEPAN, OVER LOW HEAT, UNTIL SUGAR
DISSOLVES; BRING TO THE BOIL. REDUCE HEAT;
SIMMER, UNCOVERED, WITHOUT STIRRING,
5 MINUTES. REMOVE FROM HEAT; COOL TO
ROOM TEMPERATURE. STORE IN AN AIRTIGHT
CONTAINER IN THE FRIDGE FOR UP TO 1 MONTH.

2 limes, halved
1 cup ice cubes
45ml (1½ fluid ounces) dark tequila
30ml (1 fluid ounce) orange-flavoured liqueur
30ml (1 fluid ounce) sugar syrup

1 Rub cut side of one lime half around rim of
150ml (4½-fluid ounce) margarita glass; turn glass
upside-down and dip wet rim into saucer of salt.
2 Juice limes (you need 30ml/1 fluid ounce of
juice).
3 Place ice cubes, tequila, liqueur, juice and
syrup in cocktail shaker; shake vigorously.
Strain into glass. Garnish with shredded lime
rind made using a zester.

nutritional count per serving 0.2g total fat
(0g saturated fat); 1216kJ (291 cal);
31.4g carbohydrate; 0.3g protein; 0.1g fibre

MARGARITA
PREP TIME 5 MINUTES ⚙ SERVES 1

frozen MARGARITA

PREP TIME 5 MINUTES · **SERVES 1**

2 limes, halved
1½ cups ice cubes
45ml (1½ fluid ounces) dark tequila
30ml (1 fluid ounce) orange-flavoured liqueur
30ml (1 fluid ounce) sugar syrup

1 Rub cut side of one lime half around rim of 150ml (4½-fluid ounce) margarita glass; turn glass upside-down and dip wet rim into saucer of salt.
2 Juice limes (you need 30ml/1 fluid ounce of juice).
3 Blend or process ingredients until smooth. Pour into glass; garnish with fresh mint leaves and slices of lime.

nutritional count per serving 0.2g total fat (0g saturated fat); 1216kJ (291 cal); 31.4g carbohydrate; 0.3g protein; 0.1g fibre

blood orange
MARGARITA

PREP TIME 5 MINUTES ✦ SERVES 1

2 limes, halved
1 cup ice cubes
45ml (1½ fluid ounces) dark tequila
30ml (1 fluid ounce) blood orange juice
30ml (1 fluid ounce) sugar syrup

1 Rub cut side of one lime half around rim of 260ml (8½-fluid ounce) old fashioned glass; turn glass upside-down and dip wet rim into saucer of salt.
2 Juice limes (you need 30ml/1 fluid ounce of juice).
3 Place ice cubes, tequila, juices and sugar syrup in cocktail shaker; shake vigorously. Strain into glass.

nutritional count per serving 0.2g total fat (0g saturated fat); 881kJ (210 cal); 3.1g carbohydrate; 0.4g protein; 0.1g fibre

YOU CAN BUY SUGAR SYRUP FROM MOST SUPERMARKETS OR MAKE YOUR OWN. STIR 1 CUP CASTER SUGAR WITH 1 CUP WATER IN SMALL SAUCEPAN, OVER LOW HEAT, UNTIL SUGAR DISSOLVES; BRING TO THE BOIL. REDUCE HEAT; SIMMER, UNCOVERED, WITHOUT STIRRING, 5 MINUTES. REMOVE FROM HEAT; COOL TO ROOM TEMPERATURE. STORE IN AN AIRTIGHT CONTAINER IN THE FRIDGE FOR UP TO 1 MONTH.

NOT TO BE CONFUSED WITH "SANGRIA", THE SPANISH FRUIT-LACED WINE DRINK, "SANGRITA", LOOSELY MEANING "LITTLE BLOOD", IS A TANGY, SPICY AND REFRESHING DRINK TRADITIONALLY SERVED AS A CHASER OR AS AN ACCOMPANIMENT TO GOOD-QUALITY TEQUILA – ORDERED AS TEQUILA "COMPLETO". IT WAS DESIGNED TO BE SLOWLY SIPPED ALONGSIDE A SHOOTER OF TEQUILA, CUTTING THE HARSHNESS AND COOLING THE FIRE OF THE TEQUILA. MANY OF US USUALLY ASSOCIATE TEQUILA WITH THE RITUAL OF THE "SHOT" TAKEN WITH A LICK OF SALT, FINISHED WITH A WEDGE OF LIME, BUT IN REALITY, MOST TRUE TEQUILA-LOVER'S WOULD NOT DRINK TEQUILA AS A STAND-ALONE DRINK. THEY WOULD RATHER SLOWLY SIP AND SAVOUR THE FLAVOUR OF THE DRINK, ALONGSIDE SANGRITA TO EXTRACT THE AGAVE TASTE.

125ml (4 fluid ounces) chilled tomato juice
80ml (2½ fluid ounces) chilled orange juice
40ml (1½ fluid ounces) lime juice
dash tabasco
pinch celery salt
pinch onion powder
120ml (4 fluid ounces) tequila

1 Place juices, tabasco, celery salt and onion powder in medium jug; mix well. Pour into four 80ml (2½-fluid ounce) tall shot glasses.
2 Pour tequila into four 30ml (1-fluid ounce) shot glasses; serve sangrita alongside tequila shooters.

nutritional count per serving 0.4g total fat (0g saturated fat); 322kJ (77 cal); 3.1g carbohydrate; 0.4g protein; 0.2g fibre

SANGRITA

PREP TIME 5 MINUTES ✸ SERVES 4

1 litre (4 cups) milk
3 x 5cm (2-inch) strips orange rind
1 cinnamon stick
185g (6 ounces) dark eating (semi-sweet) chocolate,
  chopped finely

1 Bring milk, rind and cinnamon to the boil in
medium saucepan. Remove from heat; stand,
covered, 5 minutes.
2 Discard rind and cinnamon. Add chocolate;
stir until smooth. Garnish with extra finely grated
dark eating chocolate.

nutritional count per serving 15.3g total fat
(9.5g saturated fat); 1133kJ (271 cal);
27.4g carbohydrate; 7.2g protein; 0.4g fibre

mexican hot
CHOCOLATE
PREP + COOK TIME 15 MINUTES (+ STANDING) SERVES 6

MEXICAN COFFEE

PREP + COOK TIME 15 MINUTES  SERVES 6

1.5 litres (6 cups) water
3 x 5cm (2-inch) strips orange rind
½ cup (45g) coarsely ground coffee beans
¼ cup (55g) raw sugar
¼ cup (55g) firmly packed light brown sugar
1 cinnamon stick
6 cloves

1 Bring 1.25 litres (5 cups) of the water to the boil in medium saucepan; stir in rind, coffee, sugars, cinnamon and cloves. Reduce heat; simmer, uncovered, 5 minutes. Remove from heat, add remaining water; stand, covered, 5 minutes.
2 Strain mixture into large heatproof jug; pour into coffee cups to serve.

nutritional count per serving 0g total fat (0g saturated fat); 297kJ (71 cal); 18.5g carbohydrate; 0.1g protein; 0.1g fibre

shredded pork and
BEAN SOUP

PREP + COOK TIME 2 HOURS 55 MINUTES ⚙ SERVES 6

1 large carrot (180g), chopped coarsely

1 stalk celery (150g), trimmed, chopped coarsely

5 cloves garlic, unpeeled, bruised

6 black peppercorns

3 sprigs fresh oregano

1 dried bay leaf

1kg (2-pound) piece pork neck

2 litres (8 cups) chicken stock

2 litres (8 cups) water

1 tablespoon olive oil

1 large red onion (300g), chopped coarsely

1 medium red capsicum (bell pepper) (200g), chopped coarsely

1 medium yellow capsicum (bell pepper) (200g), chopped coarsely

2 fresh long red chillies, sliced thinly

2 cloves garlic, crushed

810g (1½ pounds) canned chopped tomatoes

1 teaspoon ground cumin

2 tablespoons coarsely chopped fresh oregano

410g (13 ounces) canned kidney beans, drained, rinsed

1 Place carrot, celery, bruised garlic, peppercorns, oregano sprigs, bay leaf, pork, stock and the water in large saucepan; bring to the boil. Reduce heat; simmer, covered, 1 hour. Uncover; simmer 1 hour.

2 Transfer pork to medium bowl; using two forks, shred pork coarsely. Strain broth through muslin-lined sieve or colander into large heatproof bowl; discard solids.

3 Heat oil in same cleaned pan; cook onion, capsicums, chilli and crushed garlic, stirring, until vegetables soften.

4 Return pork and broth to pan with undrained tomatoes, cumin and chopped oregano; bring to the boil. Reduce heat; simmer, covered, 15 minutes. Add beans; simmer, covered, until soup is hot. Season to taste.

nutritional count per serving 7.4g total fat (1.6g saturated fat); 1490kJ (356 cal); 20.8g carbohydrate; 46.5g protein; 9.1g fibre

chipotle beef
TOSTADITAS

PREP + COOK TIME 55 MINUTES (+ STANDING) ✸ MAKES 36

2 chipotle chillies
½ cup (125ml) boiling water
12 x 17cm (6¾-inch) round white corn tortillas
vegetable oil, for deep-frying
1 tablespoon vegetable oil, extra
1 small brown onion (80g), sliced thinly
1 clove garlic, crushed
280g (9 ounces) minced (ground) beef
1 tablespoon tomato purée
1 cup (250ml) beer
¼ cup coarsely chopped fresh coriander
½ cup (120g) sour cream

1 Cover chillies with the boiling water in small heatproof bowl; stand 20 minutes.

2 Meanwhile, cut three 7cm (2¾-inch) rounds from each tortilla. Heat oil in wok; deep-fry rounds, in batches, until browned lightly. Drain on absorbent paper.

3 Drain chillies over small bowl; reserve liquid. Remove stems from chillies; discard stems. Blend or process chillies and reserved liquid until smooth.

4 Heat extra vegetable oil in medium frying pan; cook onion, stirring, until softened. Add garlic and beef; cook, stirring, until beef is changed in colour. Stir in paste, beer and chilli puree; bring to the boil. Reduce heat; simmer, uncovered, about 15 minutes or until liquid is almost evaporated. Stir in coriander. Season to taste.

5 Top each tortilla crisp with rounded teaspoon of the chipotle beef then with ½ teaspoon of the sour cream.

nutritional count per piece 3.2g total fat (1.3g saturated fat); 238kJ (57 cal); 4.3g carbohydrate; 2.4g protein; 0.6g fibre

fried oysters
WITH SALSA

PREP + COOK TIME 35 MINUTES ⚙ **MAKES 12**

1 small tomato (90g), chopped finely

½ medium yellow capsicum (bell pepper) (100g), chopped finely

½ medium red onion (85g), chopped finely

1 tablespoon finely chopped fresh coriander

1 tablespoon olive oil

1 tablespoon lime juice

1 fresh small red thai (serrano) chilli, seeded, chopped finely

12 oysters on the half shell

½ cup (85g) polenta

⅓ cup (80ml) milk

1 egg, beaten lightly

pinch cayenne pepper

vegetable oil, for deep-frying

1 Preheat oven to 180°C/350°F.

2 Combine tomato, capsicum, onion, coriander, olive oil, juice and chilli in small bowl; season to taste.

3 Remove oysters from shells; reserve oysters. Place shells on oven tray; heat in oven 5 minutes.

4 Meanwhile, combine polenta, milk, egg and pepper in small bowl.

5 Heat vegetable oil in medium saucepan. Dip oysters in batter; deep-fry oysters, in batches, until browned lightly. Drain on absorbent paper. Return oysters to shells; top with salsa.

nutritional count per oyster 5.5g total fat (1g saturated fat); 276kJ (66 cal); 6.1g carbohydrate; 2.9g protein; 0.5g fibre

1kg (2 pounds) skinless red snapper fillets
1½ cups (375ml) lime juice
¼ cup (40g) pickled sliced jalapeño chillies, drained
¼ cup (60ml) olive oil
250g (8 ounces) mixed baby tomatoes,
  chopped coarsely
¼ cup finely chopped fresh coriander
1 small red onion (100g), sliced thinly
1 clove garlic, crushed

1 Remove any remaining skin or bones from fish; cut fish into 2.5cm (1-inch) pieces.
2 Combine fish and juice in non-reactive large bowl. Cover; refrigerate overnight.
3 Drain fish; discard juice. Return fish to bowl, add remaining ingredients; toss gently to combine. Cover; refrigerate 1 hour. Season to taste.

nutritional count per serving 18.5g total fat (3.4g saturated fat); 1685kJ (403 cal); 4g carbohydrate; 52.5g protein; 1.9g fibre

CEVICHE, PRONOUNCED SE-VEE-CHAY, IS A LATIN-AMERICAN SPECIALTY. YOU NEED ABOUT 10 LIMES FOR THIS RECIPE. THE LIME JUICE "COOKS" THE FISH. FISH MUST BE MARINATED WITH THE LIME JUICE IN A NON-REACTIVE BOWL (ONE MADE FROM GLAZED PORCELAIN OR GLASS IS BEST), TO AVOID THE METALLIC TASTE THAT CAN RESULT IF MARINATING TAKES PLACE IN A STAINLESS-STEEL OR AN ALUMINIUM BOWL. ENSURE ALL OF THE FISH IS COMPLETELY COVERED WITH JUICE.

CEVICHE

PREP TIME 15 MINUTES (+ REFRIGERATION)   SERVES 4

chile
CON QUESO

PREP + COOK TIME 20 MINUTES **MAKES 2 CUPS**

2 teaspoons vegetable oil
½ small green capsicum (bell pepper) (75g),
  chopped finely
½ small brown onion (40g), chopped finely
1 tablespoon pickled sliced jalapeño chillies,
  drained, chopped finely
1 clove garlic, crushed
200g (6½ ounces) canned chopped tomatoes
250g (8 ounces) cream cheese

1 Heat oil in medium saucepan; cook capsicum,
onion, chilli and garlic, stirring, until onion softens.
Add undrained tomatoes; cook, stirring, 2 minutes.
2 Add cheese; whisk until cheese melts and
dip is smooth. Season to taste.
3 Serve hot with corn chips.

nutritional count per tablespoon 3.9g total fat
(2.3g saturated fat); 171kJ (41 cal);
0.7g carbohydrate; 1g protein; 0.2g fibre

shredded pork
CHIMICHANGA

PREP + COOK TIME 1 HOUR 50 MINUTES (+ COOLING) **SERVES 16**

500g (1 pound) diced pork
3 cloves garlic, peeled
2 black peppercorns
1 teaspoon ground cumin
3 cups (750ml) water
½ cup coarsely chopped fresh coriander
1 small red onion (80g), chopped finely
2 fresh green jalapeño chillies, seeded,
  chopped finely
8 x 20cm (8-inch) flour tortillas
vegetable oil, for deep-frying

1 Place pork, garlic, peppercorns, cumin and the water in large saucepan; bring to the boil. Reduce heat; simmer, covered, about 1 hour or until pork is tender. Cool.
2 Drain liquid from pork; discard peppercorns and liquid. Shred pork and garlic, using two forks. Combine pork mixture with coriander, onion and chilli in large bowl; season.
3 Heat tortillas according to instructions on packet. Divide pork mixture evenly between tortillas.
Roll tortillas up firmly, secure with toothpick at each end of roll.
4 Heat oil in wok or large frying pan; deep-fry tortilla rolls, in batches, until browned lightly. Drain on absorbent paper. Remove toothpicks.
5 Cut each chimichanga in half; serve with guacamole (see page 105).

nutritional count per serving 6.6g total fat (1.4g saturated fat); 544kJ (130 cal); 9.1g carbohydrate; 8.2g protein; 0.3g fibre

tortilla
LIME SOUP

PREP + COOK TIME 50 MINUTES ✪ **SERVES 4**

1 medium white onion (150g), chopped coarsely

2 cloves garlic, quartered

1 fresh long red chilli, chopped coarsely

4 medium tomatoes (600g), peeled, quartered

1 tablespoon peanut oil

¼ teaspoon ground allspice

1½ cups (375ml) chicken stock

1.25 litres (5 cups) water

2 teaspoons finely grated lime rind

¼ cup (60ml) lime juice

¼ cup (70g) tomato paste

⅓ cup (80ml) peanut oil, extra

6 x 15cm (6-inch) corn tortillas, cut into
  2cm (¾-inch) wide strips

1 medium avocado (250g), chopped finely

2 green onions (scallions), chopped finely

¼ cup coarsely chopped fresh coriander

1 Blend or process white onion, garlic, chilli and tomato until smooth.

2 Heat oil in large saucepan; cook tomato mixture and allspice, stirring, until fragrant.

3 Add stock, the water, rind, juice and paste; bring to the boil. Reduce heat; simmer, uncovered, about 15 minutes or until soup thickens. Season to taste.

4 Meanwhile, heat extra oil in medium frying pan; cook tortilla strips in batches, until golden. Drain on absorbent paper.

5 Divide tortilla strips into bowls; ladle soup over. Serve topped with combined avocado, green onion and coriander.

nutritional count per serving 33.8g total fat (6.5g saturated fat); 1764kJ (422 cal); 20.6g carbohydrate; 6.4g protein; 5.7g fibre

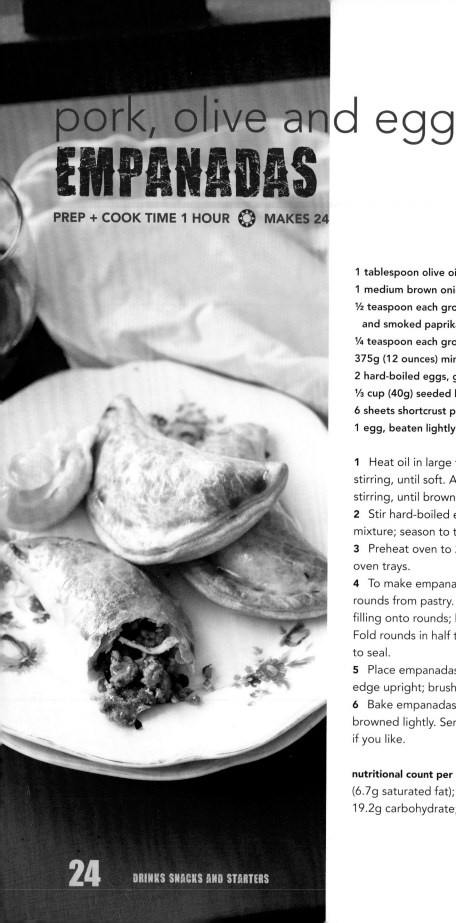

pork, olive and egg
EMPANADAS

PREP + COOK TIME 1 HOUR ✸ **MAKES 24**

1 tablespoon olive oil

1 medium brown onion (150g), chopped finely

½ teaspoon each ground cumin, ground cinnamon and smoked paprika

¼ teaspoon each ground nutmeg and ground cloves

375g (12 ounces) minced pork

2 hard-boiled eggs, grated coarsely

⅓ cup (40g) seeded black olives, chopped finely

6 sheets shortcrust pastry

1 egg, beaten lightly

1 Heat oil in large frying pan; cook onion, stirring, until soft. Add spices and pork; cook, stirring, until browned. Cool.

2 Stir hard-boiled eggs and olives into pork mixture; season to taste.

3 Preheat oven to 200°C/400°F. Oil two oven trays.

4 To make empanadas, cut 24 x 12cm (5-inch) rounds from pastry. Drop heaped tablespoons of filling onto rounds; brush edges with beaten egg. Fold rounds in half to enclose filling; pinch edges to seal.

5 Place empanadas on oven trays with sealed edge upright; brush with egg.

6 Bake empanadas about 25 minutes or until browned lightly. Serve with lemon wedges, if you like.

nutritional count per empanada 14g total fat (6.7g saturated fat); 961kJ (230 cal); 19.2g carbohydrate; 6.7g protein; 0.9g fibre

810g (1½ pounds) canned kidney beans,
   drained, rinsed
⅓ cup (85g) chunky tomato salsa
⅓ cup finely chopped fresh coriander
220g (7 ounces) corn chips
1½ cups (180g) coarsely grated cheddar cheese
2 cups (120g) finely shredded iceberg lettuce
1 small tomato (90g), chopped coarsely
½ small avocado (100g), chopped coarsely
2 tablespoons lime juice

1 Preheat oven to 220°C/425°F.
2 Combine half the beans with salsa; mash until chunky. Stir in remaining beans and coriander.
3 Spread half the chips in medium shallow baking dish; top with half the cheese and half the bean mixture. Top with remaining chips, remaining cheese then remaining bean mixture. Cook 10 minutes.
4 Place lettuce, tomato and avocado in medium bowl with juice; toss gently to combine. Season to taste.
5 Serve nachos topped with salad.

nutritional count per serving 24.5g total fat (11.6g saturated fat); 1856kJ (444 cal); 33.7g carbohydrate; 17.3g protein; 10.8g fibre

BEAN NACHOS

PREP + COOK TIME 20 MINUTES ✦ SERVES 6

crab
TOSTADAS

PREP + COOK TIME 25 MINUTES ⚙ SERVES 4

vegetable oil, for shallow-frying
4 x 15cm (6-inch) flour tortillas
410g (13 ounces) canned kidney beans, drained,
 rinsed, mashed
½ cup (60g) seeded black olives
1 cup (120g) coarsely grated cheddar cheese
1 medium tomato (150g), sliced thinly
1½ cups (90g) shredded iceberg lettuce
170g (5½ ounces) fresh cooked crab meat

AVOCADO CREAM
2 medium avocados (500g), chopped coarsely
2 tablespoons lime juice
½ cup (120g) sour cream
2 spring onions (scallions), sliced thinly
1½ tablespoons finely chopped fresh coriander

1 Make avocado cream.
2 Heat oil in medium frying pan; shallow-fry
tortillas, one at a time, until browned both sides
and crisp. Drain on absorbent paper.
3 Spread tortillas with avocado cream then
mashed beans; top with olives, cheese, tomato,
lettuce and crab meat. Season with freshly
ground black pepper.

AVOCADO CREAM Mash avocado with juice
and sour cream in medium bowl with fork until
well combined; stir in onion and coriander.
Season to taste.

nutritional count per serving 44.9g total fat
(19.1g saturated fat); 2554kJ (611 cal);
26.3g carbohydrate; 22.4g protein; 7.5g fibre

NAMED AFTER CAESAR CARDINI, THE ITALIAN-AMERICAN WHO TOSSED THE FIRST CAESAR IN MEXICO DURING THE 1920s, THIS SALAD ALWAYS CONTAINS FRESH CROUTONS, CRISP COS LETTUCE LEAVES, LIGHTLY BOILED EGGS, LEMON JUICE, OLIVE OIL, WORCESTERSHIRE SAUCE AND PARMESAN CHEESE BUT NO ONE INGREDIENT SHOULD DOMINATE.

classic
CAESAR SALAD

PREP + COOK TIME 45 MINUTES SERVES 4

½ loaf ciabatta (220g)

1 clove garlic, crushed

⅓ cup (80ml) olive oil

2 eggs

3 baby cos (romaine) lettuces, leaves separated

1 cup (80g) flaked parmesan cheese

CAESAR DRESSING

1 clove garlic, crushed

1 tablespoon dijon mustard

2 tablespoons lemon juice

2 teaspoons worcestershire sauce

2 tablespoons olive oil

1 Preheat oven to 180°C/350°F.

2 Cut bread into 2cm (¾-inch) cubes; combine garlic and oil in large bowl with bread. Toast bread on oven tray until croûtons are browned.

3 Make caesar dressing.

4 Bring water to the boil in small saucepan, add eggs; cover pan tightly, remove from heat. Remove eggs from water after 2 minutes. When cool enough to handle, break eggs into large bowl; add lettuce, mixing gently so egg coats leaves.

5 Add cheese, croûtons and dressing to bowl; toss gently to combine. Season to taste.

CAESAR DRESSING Place ingredients in screw-top jar; shake well.

nutritional count per serving 39.1g total fat (9.1g saturated fat); 2366kJ (566 cal); 33.1g carbohydrate; 18.4g protein; 5.6g fibre

THIS IS OUR VERSION OF HUEVOS RANCHEROS, OR RANCH-STYLE EGGS, WHICH TRADITIONALLY IS MADE WITH FRIED EGGS AND BEANS. FOR AN EXTRA BITE, SERVE WITH TABASCO, A FIERY SAUCE MADE FROM HOT RED CHILLIES.

scrambled eggs with
FRESH TOMATO SALSA

PREP + COOK TIME 20 MINUTES ✦ SERVES 4

3 cured chorizo sausages (500g), sliced thickly

8 eggs

½ cup (125ml) pouring cream

20g (¾ ounce) butter

4 x 15cm (6-inch) flour tortillas

1 cup (120g) coarsely grated cheddar cheese

FRESH TOMATO SALSA

2 small tomatoes (180g), chopped finely

½ small red onion (50g), chopped finely

1 tablespoon red wine vinegar

1 tablespoon olive oil

¼ cup coarsely chopped fresh coriander

1 Preheat oven to 160°C/325°F.

2 Make fresh tomato salsa.

3 Cook chorizo on heated oiled grill plate (or grill or barbecue) until well browned. Drain on absorbent paper; cover to keep warm.

4 Whisk eggs and cream in medium bowl. Melt butter in medium frying pan; cook egg mixture over low heat, stirring gently, until creamy.

5 Meanwhile, place tortillas on oven tray, sprinkle with cheese; warm in oven until cheese melts.

6 Divide tortillas between serving plates; top with egg, chorizo and salsa.

FRESH TOMATO SALSA Combine tomatoes, onion, vinegar and oil in small bowl. Cover; stand 15 minutes. Stir in coriander just before serving; season to taste.

nutritional count per serving 81.7g total fat (35.8g saturated fat); 4126kJ (987 cal); 16.2g carbohydrate; 48.2g protein; 1.9g fibre

MAINS

fish
BURRITOS

PREP + COOK TIME 30 MINUTES (+ REFRIGERATION) MAKES 8

1 cup coarsely chopped fresh coriander (cilantro)

2 teaspoons finely chopped coriander – leaf
and stem mixture

1 fresh long red chilli, chopped coarsely

1 clove garlic, quartered

1½ teaspoons sweet paprika

1 teaspoon ground cumin

⅓ cup (80ml) olive oil

800g (1½ ounces) small white fish fillets, halved

8 x 20cm (8-inch) flour tortillas

1 baby cos (romaine) lettuce (180g), leaves separated

1 lebanese cucumber (130g), sliced thinly

LIME BUTTERMILK DRESSING

¼ cup (60ml) buttermilk

1 teaspoon finely grated lime rind

2 teaspoons lime juice

1 Blend or process chopped coriander, root
and stem mixture, chilli, garlic, spices and ¼ cup
of the oil until smooth. Combine coriander
mixture and fish in large bowl. Cover; refrigerate
30 minutes.

2 Meanwhile, make lime buttermilk dressing.

3 Heat remaining oil in large frying pan; cook
fish, in batches, until browned both sides and
cooked through. Cover to keep warm.

4 Meanwhile, heat tortillas according to
instructions on packet.

5 Divide lettuce, cucumber, fish and dressing,
between tortillas; wrap to enclose filling.

LIME BUTTERMILK DRESSING Combine
ingredients in small jug; season to taste.

nutritional count per burrito 14g total fat
(2.5g saturated fat); 1267kJ (303 cal);
19g carbohydrate; 24.3g protein; 2g fibre

chilli seared tuna
with avocado cream
AND GRILLED CORN

PREP + COOK TIME 1 HOUR (+ STANDING & REFRIGERATION) SERVES 4

4 chipotle chillies

1 tablespoon olive oil

1 small brown onion (80g), chopped finely

2 cloves garlic, crushed

⅓ cup loosely packed fresh oregano leaves

2 tablespoons tomato paste

2 tablespoons water

4 x 200g (6½-ounce) tuna steaks

2 trimmed corn cobs (500g)

8 x 20cm (8-inch) flour tortillas

2 limes, cut into wedges

AVOCADO CREAM

2 small avocados (400g), chopped coarsely

½ cup (120g) sour cream

¼ cup coarsely chopped fresh coriander

1 tablespoon lime juice

1 Cover chillies with boiling water in small heatproof bowl; stand 20 minutes Drain chillies; discard stems, chop chillies coarsely.

2 Heat oil in small frying pan; cook onion and garlic, stirring, until onion softens. Stir in chilli, oregano, paste and the water; bring to the boil. Remove from heat; blend or process mixture, pulsing, until mixture forms thick paste.

3 Place fish, in single layer, in large shallow dish; using fingers, pat chilli paste onto both sides of fish. Cover; refrigerate 30 minutes.

4 Meanwhile, make avocado cream.

5 Cook corn on heated oiled grill plate (or grill or barbecue) until browned lightly and just tender. Remove from heat; slice thickly, cover to keep warm.

6 Cook undrained fish on same heated oiled grill plate until cooked as desired. Cover; stand 5 minutes. Slice fish thickly.

7 Meanwhile, heat tortillas according to instructions on packet.

8 Divide fish, corn, avocado cream and tortillas between serving plates. Serve with lime wedges.

AVOCADO CREAM Blend or process avocado and sour cream until smooth; stir in coriander and juice. Season to taste.

nutritional count per serving 49.6g total fat (17.5g saturated fat); 3883kJ (929 cal); 53.8g carbohydrate; 62.7g protein; 8.4g fibre

CEVICHE, PRONOUNCED SE-VEE-CHAY, IS A LATIN-AMERICAN SPECIALTY. THE ACIDS IN THE CITRUS MARINADE SLIGHTLY COOK THE VERY THINLY SLICED RAW SEAFOOD. USE THE FRESHEST, SASHIMI-QUALITY FISH YOU CAN FIND. RAW FISH SOLD AS SASHIMI HAS TO MEET STRINGENT GUIDELINES REGARDING ITS HANDLING AND TREATMENT AFTER LEAVING THE WATER. WE SUGGEST YOU SEEK LOCAL ADVICE FROM AUTHORITIES BEFORE EATING ANY RAW SEAFOOD.

salmon
CEVICHE SALAD

PREP TIME 25 MINUTES ✦ SERVES 4

2 medium oranges (480g)

400g (12½-ounce) piece sashimi-quality salmon, sliced thinly

175g (5½ ounces) watercress, trimmed

ORANGE AND DILL DRESSING

1 tablespoon white wine vinegar

1 tablespoon drained baby capers, rinsed

2 teaspoons finely chopped fresh dill

1 Segment oranges over small bowl; reserve ¼ cup orange juice for the dressing.

2 Make orange and dill dressing.

3 Combine salmon and half the dressing in medium bowl; stand 5 minutes.

4 Place salmon mixture in large serving bowl with remaining dressing, watercress and orange segments; toss gently to combine. Season to taste.

ORANGE AND DILL DRESSING Place vinegar, capers, dill and reserved juice in screw-top jar; shake well.

nutritional count per serving 7.3g total fat (1.6g saturated fat); 773kJ (185 cal); 7.4g carbohydrate; 21g protein; 2.6g fibre

SOAK UNSHUCKED CORN COBS IN A PAN OF COLD WATER FOR AN HOUR OR SO. PULL BACK EACH COB'S HUSK WITHOUT REMOVING IT THEN REMOVE THE SILK. BRUSH MELTED BUTTER OVER THE KERNELS THEN RE-COVER COB WITH THE HUSK. PUT CORN DIRECTLY ON YOUR HOT BARBECUE GRILL FOR ABOUT 10 MINUTES, TURNING ONCE. THE RESULT IS DELICIOUS.

char-grilled scallops with CORN SALSA

PREP + COOK TIME 45 MINUTES (+ REFRIGERATION) SERVES 4

36 scallops (900g), roe removed

2 cloves garlic, crushed

2 tablespoons lime juice

1 tablespoon olive oil

2 corn cobs (800g), trimmed

200g (6½ ounces) grape tomatoes, halved

1 large avocado (320g), chopped coarsely

1 medium red onion (170g), chopped finely

1 medium green capsicum (bell pepper) (200g), chopped finely

2 fresh small red thai (serrano) chillies, chopped finely

¼ cup coarsely chopped fresh coriander

8 x 15cm (6-inch) white corn tortillas

2 limes, cut into wedges

LIME DRESSING

¼ cup (60ml) lime juice

½ teaspoon ground cumin

2 teaspoons olive oil

1 Combine scallops, garlic, juice and oil in large bowl. Cover; refrigerate 3 hours or overnight.

2 Make lime dressing.

3 Cook corn on heated oiled grill plate (or grill or barbecue) until browned lightly and just tender. Using sharp knife, cut corn kernels from cobs. Combine corn kernels in large bowl with tomato, avocado, onion, capsicum, chilli, coriander and dressing; season to taste.

4 Cook drained scallops, in batches, on same heated grill plate until browned lightly and cooked as desired. Remove from heat; cover to keep warm.

5 Using tongs, place tortillas, one at a time, briefly, on same grill plate to lightly brown both sides (work quickly as tortillas toughen if overcooked). Wrap tortillas in tea towel to keep warm.

6 Serve scallops with salsa, tortillas and lime wedges.

LIME DRESSING Place ingredients in screw-top jar; shake well.

nutritional count per serving 24.1g total fat (4.4g saturated fat); 2416kJ (578 cal); 50.6g carbohydrate; 37.8g protein; 12.2g fibre

1 tablespoon olive oil

500g (1 pound) minced (ground) beef

1 medium brown onion (150g), chopped finely

1 clove garlic, crushed

1 teaspoon ground cumin

¼ teaspoon chilli powder

400g (12½ ounces) canned chopped tomatoes

½ cup (125ml) water

410g (13 ounces) canned kidney beans,
   drained, rinsed

4 x 20cm (8-inch) flour tortillas

1 cup (120g) coarsely grated cheddar cheese

1 teaspoon hot paprika

¾ cup (180g) sour cream

¼ cup fresh coriander leaves

1 Heat oil in medium frying pan; cook beef, stirring, until browned. Add onion, garlic, cumin and chilli powder; cook, stirring, until onion softens. Stir in undrained tomatoes, the water and beans; simmer, uncovered, about 15 minutes or until mixture thickens. Remove from heat; season to taste.

2 Preheat oven to 200°C/400°F.

3 Divide warm beef filling between tortillas, roll to enclose filling; secure with toothpicks.

4 Place filled tortillas on oiled oven tray; sprinkle with cheese and paprika.

5 Bake burritos about 10 minutes or until heated through. Remove toothpicks; serve topped with sour cream, coriander and, if you like, guacamole (see page 105).

nutritional count per burrito 45g total fat (24g saturated fat); 3022kJ (723 cal); 34.1g carbohydrate; 42.4g protein; 7.3g fibre

beef
BURRITOS

PREP + COOK TIME 55 MINUTES ✺ MAKES 4

pork and cheese
QUESADILLAS

PREP + COOK TIME 50 MINUTES ✷ SERVES 4

1 tablespoon olive oil
500g (1 pound) minced pork
1 medium green capsicum (bell pepper) (200g),
  chopped finely
1 fresh long red chilli, chopped finely
1 clove garlic, crushed
½ cup coarsely chopped fresh coriander
8 x 20cm (8-inch) flour tortillas
2 tablespoons olive oil, extra
2 cups (240g) coarsely grated cheddar cheese

1 Heat oil in large frying pan; cook pork, stirring,
until browned. Add capsicum, chilli and garlic;
cook, stirring, until fragrant. Remove from heat;
stir in coriander, season to taste.
2 Brush one side of each tortilla with extra oil.
Spread pork mixture evenly over half the tortillas,
oiled side down; sprinkle with cheese. Top with
remaining tortillas, oiled side up.
3 Cook quesadillas, in batches, in heated
sandwich press or frying pan until browned
lightly. Cut quesadillas into quarters; serve with
guacamole (see page 105), if you like.

nutritional count per serving 47.5g total fat
(19g saturated fat); 3189kJ (763 cal);
36.3g carbohydrate; 46.8g protein; 2.7g fibre

chicken
ENCHILADAS

PREP + COOK TIME 1 HOUR 25 MINUTES ⊛ **MAKES 10**

3 chipotle chillies
1 cup (250ml) boiling water
500g (1 pound) chicken breast fillets
1 tablespoon vegetable oil
1 large red onion (300g), chopped finely
2 cloves garlic, crushed
1 teaspoon ground cumin
1 tablespoon tomato paste
800g (1½ pounds) canned chopped tomatoes
1 tablespoon finely chopped fresh oregano
⅔ cup (160g) sour cream
1½ cups (240g) coarsely grated cheddar cheese
10 x 15cm (6-inch) flour tortillas

1 Cover chillies with the boiling water in small heatproof bowl; stand 20 minutes. Discard stems from chillies. Blend or process chillies with soaking liquid until smooth.

2 Meanwhile, place chicken in medium saucepan of boiling water; return to the boil. Reduce heat; simmer, covered, about 10 minutes or until chicken is cooked through. Remove chicken from poaching liquid; cool 10 minutes. Discard poaching liquid
(or keep for another use); shred chicken finely.

3 Preheat oven to 180°C/350°F. Oil shallow rectangular 3-litre (12-cup) ovenproof dish.

4 Heat oil in large frying pan; cook onion, stirring, until softened. Reserve half of the onion in small bowl.

5 Add garlic and cumin to remaining onion in pan; cook, stirring, until fragrant. Add chilli mixture, tomato paste, undrained tomatoes and oregano; bring to the boil. Reduce heat; simmer, uncovered, 1 minute. Remove sauce from heat. Season to taste.

6 Meanwhile, combine shredded chicken, reserved onion, half the sour cream and a third of the cheese in medium bowl.

7 Heat tortillas according to instructions on packet. Dip tortillas, one at a time, in tomato sauce in pan; place on board. Place ¼ cup of the chicken mixture along edge of each tortilla; roll enchiladas to enclose filling.

8 Spread ½ cup tomato sauce into dish. Place enchiladas, seam-side down, in dish (they should fit snugly, without overcrowding). Pour remaining tomato sauce over enchiladas; sprinkle with remaining cheese.

9 Cook enchiladas, in oven, uncovered, about 15 minutes or until cheese melts and enchiladas are heated through. Serve with remaining sour cream; sprinkle with coriander (cilantro) leaves, if you like.

nutritional count per enchilada 20g total fat (10.5g saturated fat); 1588kJ (379 cal); 25g carbohydrate; 22.3g protein; 3.3g fibre

SALTED COD, ALSO CALLED SALT COD, BACCALA, BACALHAU,
BACALAO AND MORUE, IS AVAILABLE FROM ITALIAN, SPANISH AND
PORTUGUESE DELICATESSENS AND SOME SPECIALTY FOOD STORES.
IT NEEDS TO BE DE-SALTED AND REHYDRATED BEFORE USE.

salt cod with
ROASTED TOMATOES

PREP + COOK TIME 50 MINUTES (+ REFRIGERATION & STANDING) **SERVES 6**

1.5kg (3 pounds) salted cod fillets, skin on

6 large tomatoes (1.3kg)

½ cup (125ml) olive oil

1 medium brown onion (150g), chopped coarsely

2 ancho chillies

¼ cup (60ml) boiling water

500g (1 pound) baby new potatoes, halved

4 medium brown onions (600g), chopped finely

6 cloves garlic, crushed

1 teaspoon smoked paprika

1 cup (150g) pimiento-stuffed green olives

½ cup coarsely chopped fresh flat-leaf parsley

1 Rinse fish under cold water to remove excess
salt. Place fish in large bowl, cover with cold
water; refrigerate, covered, overnight, changing
the water three or four times. Drain fish; discard
water.

2 Preheat oven to 200°C/400°F.

3 Remove cores from tops of tomatoes; cut a
small cross in the skin at base of each tomato.
Place on oiled oven tray, drizzle with 1
tablespoon of the oil; roast 15 minutes or until
tomatoes begin to soften. When cool enough to
handle, peel away skins.

4 Meanwhile, place fish in large saucepan with
coarsely chopped onion, cover with water; bring
to the boil. Reduce heat; simmer, uncovered,
15 minutes or until fish is cooked. Drain fish;
discard liquid and onion. Remove skin and bones
from fish; flake fish into 4cm (1½-inch) pieces.

5 Cover chillies with the boiling water in small
heatproof bowl; stand 20 minutes. Drain chillies;
discard stems and seeds, chop chillies coarsely.
Blend or process tomatoes and chillies until
smooth.

6 Boil, steam or microwave potatoes until
tender; drain.

7 Heat remaining oil in large frying pan; cook
finely chopped onion and garlic, stirring, until
onion is softened and browned lightly. Add
paprika; cook, stirring, 1 minute. Add tomato
mixture, fish, potatoes, olives and parsley; season
to taste, stir gently until heated through.

nutritional count per serving 3.8g total fat
(0.6g saturated fat); 589kJ (141 cal);
3.1g carbohydrate; 22.7g protein; 1.2g fibre

SERVING SUGGESTION
Serve with crusty bread to mop up
the juices, steamed green beans
and rice or a green salad.

CHICKEN MOLE

PREP + COOK TIME 1 HOUR 20 MINUTES SERVES 6

6 x 500g (1-pound) small chickens
⅓ cup (50g) plain (all-purpose) flour
¼ cup (60ml) olive oil
1 medium brown onion (150g), chopped finely
2 cloves garlic, crushed
1 cinnamon stick
½ teaspoon ground nutmeg
¼ teaspoon ground cloves
800g (1½ pounds) canned crushed tomatoes
1 large red capsicum (bell pepper) (350g),
  sliced thinly
1 cup (250ml) dry white wine
60g (2 ounces) dark eating (semi-sweet) chocolate,
  chopped finely
⅓ cup coarsely chopped fresh flat-leaf parsley

1 Rinse chickens under cold water; pat dry with absorbent paper. Using kitchen scissors, cut along sides of chickens' backbones; discard backbones. Halve chickens along breastbones then cut each half into two pieces.
2 Coat chicken in flour; shake off excess. Heat oil in large frying pan; cook chicken, in batches, until browned. Drain on absorbent paper.
3 Cook onion and garlic in same pan, stirring, until onion softens. Add spices; cook, stirring, until fragrant.
4 Return chicken to pan with undrained tomatoes, capsicum and wine; simmer, covered, 20 minutes. Uncover; simmer about 20 minutes or until chicken is tender and sauce thickens slightly. Add chocolate; cook, stirring, until smooth. Discard cinnamon stick; season to taste. Serve chicken with sauce; sprinkle with parsley.

nutritional count per serving 51.9g total fat (15.3g saturated fat); 3294kJ (788 cal); 20.1g carbohydrate; 52.8g protein; 3.3g fibre

marinated
CHILLI CHICKENS

PREP + COOK TIME 1 HOUR 20 MINUTES (+ REFRIGERATION) SERVES 8

4 x 500g (1-pound) small chickens

2 small brown onions (200g), chopped coarsely

8 cloves garlic, peeled

8 fresh long red chillies

⅓ cup (80ml) red wine vinegar

1 tablespoon ground cumin

2 tablespoons olive oil

4 medium ripe tomatoes (750g), quartered

1 Rinse chickens under cold water; pat dry with absorbent paper. Using kitchen scissors, cut along sides of chickens' backbones; discard backbones. Halve chickens along breastbones.

2 Blend or process onion, garlic, chillies, vinegar and cumin until almost smooth.

3 Heat oil in large frying pan, add onion mixture; cook, stirring, until fragrant.

4 Blend or process tomatoes until smooth, add to onion mixture; cook, stirring, until mixture boils. Reduce heat; simmer, uncovered, stirring, about 20 minutes or until thickened. Season to taste. Brush chickens with half of the chilli sauce; cover, refrigerate 3 hours.

5 Preheat oven to 220°C/425°F.

6 Place chickens, skin-side up, on oiled rack in large shallow baking dish; roast about 30 minutes or until cooked through.

7 Serve chicken with remaining chilli sauce and, if you like, green salad leaves, and grilled corn and zucchini salsa (see page 102).

nutritional count per serving 19.3g total fat (5.1g saturated fat); 1300kJ (311 cal); 3.6g carbohydrate; 29.7g protein; 2g fibre

chicken in pumpkin seed and
TOMATILLO SAUCE

PREP + COOK TIME 1 HOUR ✸ SERVES 6

SERVING SUGGESTION
Serve with steamed rice, lime wedges and fresh coriander (cilantro) leaves.

2 medium tomatoes (300g), quartered

1 medium brown onion (150g), quartered

2 tablespoons olive oil

6 chicken thigh cutlets (1.2kg)

6 chicken drumsticks (900g)

1½ cups (375ml) chicken stock

1 cup (200g) pumpkin seed kernels (pepitas), roasted

2 tablespoons pickled sliced jalapeño chillies, drained

½ cup (125g) drained chopped tomatillos

2 cloves garlic, quartered

½ cup firmly packed fresh coriander leaves

⅓ cup coarsely chopped fresh chives

½ teaspoon ground cumin

1 Preheat oven to 200°C/400°F.

2 Place tomato and onion on oiled oven tray; drizzle with half the oil. Roast, uncovered, about 25 minutes or until vegetables soften. Cool.

3 Meanwhile, place chicken in large saucepan with stock; bring to the boil. Reduce heat; simmer, covered, about 20 minutes or until chicken is just cooked through. Remove chicken from pan; reserve 1¼ cups of stock.

4 Blend or process pumpkin seed kernels until a fine powder; sift powder through fine sieve. Blend or process pumpkin seed powder with tomato and onion mixture, chilli, tomatillos, garlic, coriander, chives and cumin until smooth.

5 Heat remaining oil in same cleaned pan; cook chicken, in batches, until browned. Remove from pan. Add pumpkin seed mixture to pan; cook, stirring, 3 minutes. Add reserved stock; simmer, uncovered, 2 minutes. Return chicken to pan; simmer, uncovered, until chicken is heated through. Season to taste.

nutritional count per serving 52g total fat (13g saturated fat); 2959kJ (708 cal); 8.6g carbohydrate; 50.1g protein; 5g fibre

POMEGRANATE PULP CONSISTS OF THE SEEDS
AND THE EDIBLE PULP SURROUNDING THEM;
IT HAS A TANGY SWEET-SOUR FLAVOUR.

chicken in almond
POMEGRANATE SAUCE

PREP + COOK TIME 35 MINUTES SERVES 4

2 medium pomegranates (640g)

1½ cups (375ml) water

⅓ cup (75g) firmly packed light brown sugar

2 tablespoons olive oil

4 x 200g (6½-ounce) chicken breast fillets

1 large brown onion (200g), sliced thickly

2 cloves garlic, crushed

1 tablespoon plain (all-purpose) flour

1 teaspoon each sweet paprika, ground cumin and
 ground coriander

½ teaspoon ground cinnamon

pinch chilli powder

½ cup (125ml) chicken stock

⅓ cup (55g) blanched almonds, roasted

⅓ cup coarsely chopped fresh coriander

1 Cut pomegranates in half, scoop out pulp. Reserve about ⅓ cup pulp. Place remaining pulp in small saucepan with the water and sugar; stir over heat, without boiling, until sugar dissolves. Simmer, uncovered, 5 minutes; strain syrup into medium heatproof jug.

2 Heat half the oil in large frying pan; cook chicken, in batches, until browned. Remove from pan.

3 Heat remaining oil in same pan; cook onion and garlic, stirring, until onion softens. Add flour and spices; cook, stirring, about 1 minute or until mixture is just browned and dry. Gradually stir in stock and pomegranate syrup; cook, stirring, until mixture boils and thickens slightly.

4 Return chicken to pan; simmer, covered, about 5 minutes or until cooked through. Stir in reserved pomegranate pulp, nuts and coriander; season to taste.

nutritional count per serving 28g total fat (5.3g saturated fat); 2366kJ (566 cal); 29.3g carbohydrate; 47.8g protein; 4.8g fibre

2 tablespoons vegetable oil

1 medium brown onion (150g), chopped finely

1 clove garlic, crushed

1 teaspoon each ground cumin and ground coriander

½ teaspoon chilli powder

750g (1½ pounds) minced beef

800g (1½ pounds) canned crushed tomatoes

410g (13 ounces) canned mexican-style beans, drained

⅓ cup (80g) sour cream

⅓ cup loosely packed fresh coriander leaves

1 Heat half the oil in large frying pan; cook onion, garlic and spices, stirring, until onion softens.

2 Combine beef with onion mixture in medium bowl; season. Using hands, roll level tablespoons of mixture into balls.

3 Heat remaining oil in same pan; cook meatballs, in batches, until browned all over. Remove from pan.

4 Add tomato and beans to same pan; bring to the boil. Reduce heat; simmer, uncovered, about 5 minutes or until mixture thickens slightly. Return meatballs to pan; simmer, uncovered, about 10 minutes or until meatballs are cooked through. Season to taste.

5 Serve meatballs with sour cream, coriander and, if you like, guacamole (see page 105).

nutritional count per serving 32.2g total fat (13.4g saturated fat); 2349kJ (562 cal); 20.4g carbohydrate; 44.6g protein; 7.8g fibre

SERVING SUGGESTION
Serve with flour tortillas to scoop up the sauce.

ALBONDIGAS

PREP + COOK TIME 50 MINUTES ✿ SERVES 4

blackened
STEAK SALAD

PREP + COOK TIME 30 MINUTES ⊛ **SERVES 4**

4 x 15cm (6-inch) flour tortillas

500g (1-pound) beef fillet

2 teaspoons hot paprika

1 teaspoon ground black pepper

½ teaspoon cayenne pepper

¼ teaspoon each dried oregano and dried thyme

3 medium tomatoes (450g), chopped finely

1 large green capsicum (bell pepper) (350g),
  chopped finely

1 lebanese cucumber (130g), seeded, chopped finely

½ cup coarsely chopped fresh mint

1 tablespoon olive oil

1 tablespoon balsamic vinegar

1 clove garlic, crushed

1 lime, cut into wedges

1 Cook tortillas on heated oiled grill plate (or
grill or barbecue) both sides until browned lightly.
Break into coarse pieces.
2 Rub beef with combined spices, season; cook
on heated oiled grill plate (or grill or barbecue),
turning, until browned and cooked as desired.
Cover beef; stand 5 minutes then slice thinly.
3 Place beef and tortillas pieces in large bowl
with remaining ingredients; toss gently to combine,
season to taste. Serve with lime wedges.

nutritional count per serving 13.7g total fat
(4g saturated fat); 1304kJ (312 cal);
14.5g carbohydrate; 30.6g protein; 3.4g fibre

SERVING SUGGESTION
Serve with steamed rice; top with
thinly sliced white onion and
fresh coriander (cilantro) leaves.

chilli
CON CARNE

PREP + COOK TIME 3 HOURS 45 MINUTES (+ STANDING) ✶ **SERVES 8**

1 cup (200g) dried kidney beans

1.5kg (3 pounds) beef chuck steak

2 litres (8 cups) water

1 tablespoon olive oil

2 medium brown onions (300g), chopped coarsely

2 cloves garlic, crushed

2 teaspoons each ground coriander, ground cumin
  and sweet paprika

½ teaspoon cayenne pepper

800g (1½ pounds) canned chopped tomatoes

2 tablespoons tomato paste

4 spring onions (scallions), chopped coarsely

2 tablespoons coarsely chopped fresh coriander

⅓ cup (65g) finely chopped pickled jalapeño chillies

1 Place beans in medium bowl, cover with water; stand overnight. Drain.

2 Place beef and the water in large saucepan; bring to the boil. Reduce heat; simmer, covered, 1½ hours.

3 Drain beef in large muslin-lined strainer over large heatproof bowl; reserve 3½ cups (875ml) of the cooking liquid. Using two forks, shred beef.

4 Heat oil in same pan; cook brown onion and garlic, stirring, until onion softens. Add spices; cook, stirring, until fragrant. Add beans, undrained tomatoes, paste and 2 cups of the reserved cooking liquid; bring to the boil. Reduce heat; simmer, covered, 1 hour.

5 Add beef and remaining reserved cooking liquid to pan; simmer, covered, about 30 minutes or until beans are tender. Remove from heat; stir in green onions, coriander and chilli. Season to taste.

nutritional count per serving 11.5g total fat
(4g saturated fat); 1513kJ (362 cal);
15.1g carbohydrate; 45.4g protein; 7.8g fibre

A QUESADILLA (FROM QUESO, THE SPANISH WORD FOR CHEESE) IS A TORTILLA "SANDWICH" CONTAINING CHEESE AND ANY OF A WIDE NUMBER OF SPICY FILLING INGREDIENTS, WHICH IS GRILLED, FRIED OR TOASTED AND USUALLY SERVED WITH SALSA. WE COOKED THESE QUESADILLAS IN A FRYING PAN BUT YOU CAN COOK QUESADILLAS, ONE AT A TIME, IN A HEATED SANDWICH PRESS, IF YOU HAVE ONE.

corn and goat's cheese
QUESADILLAS

PREP + COOK TIME 30 MINUTES ✦ **SERVES 4**

2 corn cobs (800g), trimmed

240g (7½ ounces) soft goat's cheese

8 x 20cm (8-inch) flour tortillas

½ cup (100g) drained char-grilled red capsicum (bell pepper), sliced thinly

2 tablespoons pickled sliced jalapeño chillies, drained

⅓ cup coarsely chopped fresh coriander

20g (¾ ounce) butter

40g (1½ ounces) baby spinach leaves

1 lime, cut into wedges

1 Cook corn on heated oiled grill plate (or grill or barbecue) until browned lightly and tender; when cool enough to handle, cut kernels from cobs.

2 Spread cheese over tortillas. Top 4 of the tortillas with corn, capsicum, chilli and coriander, season; top with remaining tortillas. Press around edges firmly to seal quesadillas.

3 Melt butter in medium frying pan; cook quesadillas, one at a time, until browned both sides and heated through.

4 Serve quesadillas with spinach and lime wedges.

nutritional count per serving 21.7g total fat (10g saturated fat); 2169kJ (519 cal); 57g carbohydrate; 19.8g protein; 8.6g fibre

lamb shanks in
CHILLI SAUCE

PREP + COOK TIME 2 HOURS 30 MINUTES ☀ **SERVES 4**

3 ancho chillies

1 cup (250ml) boiling water

1 tablespoon olive oil

8 french-trimmed lamb shanks (2kg)

1 medium brown onion (150g), chopped finely

3 cloves garlic, crushed

1 teaspoon ground cumin

½ teaspoon ground coriander

2 sprigs fresh thyme

1 litre (4 cups) beef stock

2 cups (500ml) water, extra

2 dried bay leaves

⅓ cup loosely packed fresh coriander
  leaves

2 limes, cut into wedges

1 Cover chillies with the boiling water in small heatproof bowl; stand 20 minutes. Discard stems and seeds from chillies; blend or process chillies with soaking liquid until smooth.

2 Heat oil in large saucepan; cook lamb, in batches, until browned. Remove from pan; drain on absorbent paper.

3 Drain fat from pan, add onion and garlic to same pan; cook, stirring, until onion softens. Add spices and chilli mixture; cook, stirring, until fragrant.

4 Return lamb to pan with thyme, stock, the extra water and bay leaves; bring to the boil. Reduce heat; simmer, covered, about 1½ hours, skimming fat from surface occasionally, or until lamb is tender and almost falling off the bone. Uncover; simmer about 20 minutes or until sauce thickens slightly. Discard thyme and bay leaves; season to taste.

5 Divide lamb between serving bowls; top with coriander. Serve with lime wedges and crusty bread.

nutritional count per serving 9.7g total fat (3.2g saturated fat); 1559kJ (373 cal); 4.9g carbohydrate; 65.3g protein; 1.1g fibre

spiced grilled beef
WITH CHILLI BEANS

PREP + COOK TIME 1 HOUR 45 MINUTES (+ STANDING)   **SERVES 4**

PASILLA (PRONOUNCED PAH-SEE-YAH) CHILLIES, ALSO CALLED "CHILE NEGRO" BECAUSE OF THEIR DARK BROWN COLOUR, ARE THE WRINKLED, DRIED VERSION OF FRESH CHILACA CHILLIES. ABOUT 20CM (8 INCHES) IN LENGTH, A PASILLA IS ONLY MILDLY HOT, BUT POSSESSES A RICH FLAVOUR THAT ADDS SMOKY DEPTH TO THE OVERALL RECIPE.

2 cups (400g) dried black beans

2 pasilla chillies (10g)

¼ cup (60ml) boiling water

2 tablespoons olive oil

1 medium brown onion (150g), chopped finely

3 cloves garlic, crushed

¼ cup (70g) tomato purée

4 medium tomatoes (600g), chopped coarsely

½ cup (125ml) water

2 tablespoons lime juice

2 tablespoons light brown sugar

1 tablespoon dried marjoram

2 teaspoons smoked paprika

1kg (2 pounds) beef rump steak

8 x 20cm (8-inch) flour tortillas

1 small iceberg lettuce, trimmed, shredded finely

1 small red onion (100g), sliced thinly

⅓ cup firmly packed fresh coriander leaves

⅔ cup (160g) sour cream

1 Place beans in medium bowl, cover with water; stand overnight, drain.

2 Cook beans in large saucepan of boiling water, uncovered, until tender; drain. Rinse under cold water; drain.

3 Meanwhile, cover chillies with the boiling water in small heatproof bowl; stand 20 minutes. Discard stalks from chillies. Blend or process chillies with soaking liquid until smooth.

4 Heat half the oil in large saucepan; cook brown onion and garlic, stirring, until onion softens. Add chilli mixture, paste, tomato, the water, juice and sugar; bring to the boil. Remove from heat; blend or process mixture until smooth.

5 Return chilli mixture to pan; add beans, simmer, covered, 20 minutes. Uncover; simmer about 10 minutes or until sauce thickens. Season to taste.

6 Meanwhile, combine marjoram, paprika and remaining oil in large bowl; add beef, turn to coat in mixture, season. Cook beef on heated oiled grill plate (or grill or barbecue) until browned both sides and cooked as desired. Cover beef; stand 10 minutes then slice thinly.

7 Meanwhile, heat tortillas according to instructions on packet.

8 Serve tortillas topped with chilli beans, red onion, lettuce, beef, coriander and sour cream.

nutritional count per serving 49.8g total fat (20.4g saturated fat); 5158kJ (1234 cal); 96.2g carbohydrate; 92g protein; 21.4g fibre

chilli lamb roasts with
BLACK BEAN SALAD

PREP + COOK TIME 1 HOUR 20 MINUTES (+ STANDING & REFRIGERATION) **SERVES 4**

1 cup (200g) dried black beans
2 mini lamb roasts (700g)
¼ cup (60ml) olive oil
1 large brown onion (200g), chopped finely
1 clove garlic, crushed
1 fresh long green chilli, chopped finely
1 teaspoon ground cumin
2 tablespoons red wine vinegar
1 large tomato (220g), seeded, chopped coarsely
½ cup firmly packed fresh coriander leaves
3 spring onions (scallions), sliced thinly
2 tablespoons lime juice

CHILLI MARINADE

3 fresh long green chillies, chopped finely
3 spring onions (scallions), chopped finely
2 cloves garlic, crushed
1 teaspoon each ground allspice and dried thyme
1 teaspoon white (granulated) sugar
1 tablespoon worcestershire sauce
1 tablespoon lime juice

1 Place beans in medium bowl, cover with water; stand overnight.
2 Combine ingredients for chilli marinade in large bowl; add lamb, rub all over with marinade. Cover; refrigerate overnight.
3 Preheat oven to 180°C/350°F.
4 Drain beans; rinse under cold water. Cook beans in medium saucepan of boiling water, uncovered, about 20 minutes or until tender; drain.
5 Meanwhile, heat half the oil in medium flameproof casserole dish; cook lamb, uncovered, until browned all over. Roast lamb, uncovered, in oven, about 20 minutes or until cooked as desired. Cover lamb; stand 10 minutes then slice thickly.
6 Meanwhile, heat remaining oil in same cleaned saucepan; cook brown onion, garlic, chilli and cumin, stirring, until onion softens. Add vinegar; cook, stirring, until liquid evaporates. Remove from heat.
7 Combine onion mixture, beans, tomato, coriander, green onion and juice in large bowl; season to taste.
8 Serve lamb with salad.

nutritional count per serving 30.2g total fat (9g saturated fat); 2353kJ (563 cal); 22.4g carbohydrate; 49.8g protein; 12.8g fibre

BLACK BEANS, ALSO KNOWN AS TURTLE BEANS, ARE A COMMON INGREDIENT IN CARIBBEAN AND LATIN AMERICAN SOUPS, SALSAS AND SALADS. THEY ARE NOT THE SAME AS CHINESE BLACK BEANS, WHICH ARE FERMENTED SOY BEANS. THEY ARE AVAILABLE FROM GREENGROCERS AND DELICATESSENS.

LAMB FAJITAS

PREP + COOK TIME 45 MINUTES SERVES 4

600g (1¼ pounds) lamb strips

3 cloves garlic, crushed

¼ cup (60ml) lemon juice

2 teaspoons ground cumin

1 tablespoon olive oil

1 large red capsicum (bell pepper) (350g), sliced thickly

1 large green capsicum (bell pepper) (350g), sliced thickly

1 medium yellow capsicum (bell pepper) (200g), sliced thickly

1 large red onion (300g), sliced thickly

8 x 20cm (8-inch) flour tortillas

GUACAMOLE

1 large avocado (320g), chopped coarsely

¼ cup finely chopped fresh coriander

1 tablespoon lime juice

1 small white onion (80g), chopped finely

SALSA CRUDA

2 medium tomatoes (300g), seeded, chopped finely

1 fresh long green chilli, chopped finely

½ cup coarsely chopped fresh coriander

1 clove garlic, crushed

1 small white onion (80g), chopped finely

2 tablespoons lime juice

1 Combine lamb, garlic, juice, cumin and oil in large bowl. Cover; refrigerate.

2 Make guacamole.

3 Make salsa cruda.

4 Cook lamb, in batches, in heated oiled frying pan, stirring, until browned all over and cooked as desired. Remove from pan. Cover to keep warm.

5 Cook capsicums and onion, in batches, in same pan, stirring, until just softened. Remove from pan.

6 Meanwhile, heat tortillas according to instructions on packet.

7 Return lamb and capsicum mixture to pan; stir gently over medium heat until hot.

8 Divide lamb mixture between serving plates; serve with tortillas, guacamole and salsa cruda.

GUACAMOLE Gently combine ingredients in small bowl; season to taste.

SALSA CRUDA Combine ingredients in small bowl; season to taste.

nutritional count per serving 37.5g total fat (10.4g saturated fat); 3227kJ (772 cal); 62.3g carbohydrate; 45.8g protein; 8.4g fibre

seasoned roast pork with prune sauce
(recipe page 72)

seasoned roast pork
WITH PRUNE SAUCE

PREP + COOK TIME 2 HOURS (+ STANDING) ⚙ **SERVES 8**

(photograph page 71)

2kg (4-pound) boneless loin of pork, rind on

SEASONING

1 tablespoon olive oil

1 medium brown onion (150g), chopped finely

2 cloves garlic, crushed

2 medium tomatoes (300g), seeded, chopped finely

½ cup (75g) raisins

½ cup (80g) blanched almonds, chopped finely

300g (9½ ounces) minced (ground) pork and veal

1 cup (70g) stale breadcrumbs

PRUNE SAUCE

1 medium brown onion (150g), quartered

1 medium tomato (150g), quartered

3 cloves garlic, unpeeled

2 tablespoons olive oil

2 chipotle chillies

⅓ cup (55g) blanched almonds

¾ cup (125g) seeded prunes

4 cloves

1 teaspoon ground cinnamon

2 tablespoons cider vinegar

1 cup (250ml) chicken stock

1 Make seasoning.

2 Preheat oven to 220°C/425°F.

3 Place pork, fat-side down, on board; slice through thickest part of the pork horizontally, without cutting through the other side. Open pork out to form one large piece. Press seasoning mixture along one long side of pork; roll pork to enclose seasoning. Tie with kitchen string at 2cm (¾-inch) intervals; place pork on wire rack in large shallow baking dish. Roast pork, uncovered, 30 minutes.

4 Reduce oven to 200°C/400°F. Roast pork, covered, about 1 hour or until cooked through.

5 Meanwhile, make prune sauce.

6 Remove pork from dish; cover pork loosely with foil, stand 15 minutes then slice thinly.

7 Serve pork with prune sauce.

SEASONING Heat oil in large frying pan; cook onion and garlic, stirring, until onion softens. Add tomato, raisins and nuts; simmer, uncovered, about 5 minutes or until thick. Cool. Combine tomato mixture, minced pork and veal, and breadcrumbs in medium bowl, season; mix well.

PRUNE SAUCE Preheat oven to 200°C/400°F. Place onion, tomato and garlic on oiled oven tray; drizzle with half the oil. Roast, uncovered, about 25 minutes or until vegetables soften. When cool enough to handle, peel tomato and garlic. Meanwhile, remove stems, seeds and membranes from chillies; chop chillies coarsely. Cover chillies with boiling water in small heatproof bowl; stand 20 minutes. Drain. Heat remaining oil in large frying pan; cook nuts, prunes and spices, stirring, until nuts are browned lightly. Blend or process nut mixture and vinegar until mixture forms a thick paste. Add drained chillies, onion, tomato and garlic; process until smooth. Add chilli mixture and stock to same heated pan; simmer, stirring occasionally, until sauce is heated through. Season to taste.

nutritional count per serving 33.4g total fat (7.5g saturated fat); 2796kJ (669 cal); 23.6g carbohydrate; 66.9g protein; 4.9g fibre

barbecued corn with
CHUNKY SALSA AND RICE

PREP + COOK TIME 50 MINUTES (+ REFRIGERATION) ⬡ **SERVES 4**

4 untrimmed corn cobs (1.6kg)

2 teaspoons peanut oil

2 cloves garlic, crushed

1 small white onion (80g), chopped finely

1 small red capsicum (bell pepper) (150g), chopped finely

1 fresh long red chilli, chopped finely

1½ cups (300g) white medium-grain rice

1 cup (250ml) vegetable stock

1 cup (250ml) water

CHUNKY SALSA

3 medium tomatoes (450g), chopped coarsely

1 small white onion (80g), chopped finely

¼ cup (60g) pickled sliced jalapeño chillies, drained

½ cup coarsely chopped fresh coriander

1 clove garlic, crushed

2 tablespoons lime juice

1 Gently peel husk down corn cob, keeping husk attached at base. Remove as much silk as possible then bring husk back over cob to re-wrap and enclose completely. Place corn in large bowl, add enough cold water to completely submerge corn.

2 Heat oil in medium saucepan; cook garlic, onion, capsicum and chilli, stirring, until onion softens. Add rice; cook, stirring, 1 minute. Add stock and the water; bring to the boil. Reduce heat; simmer, covered, about 20 minutes or until rice is just tender. Remove from heat; fluff rice with fork, season to taste.

3 Meanwhile, drain corn. Cook corn on heated oiled grill plate (or grill or barbecue) about 25 minutes or until corn is tender, turning occasionally.

4 Make chunky salsa.

5 Serve corn with rice and salsa.

CHUNKY SALSA Combine ingredients in medium bowl; season to taste.

nutritional count per serving 6.7g total fat (0.9g saturated fat); 2541kJ (608 cal); 114g carbohydrate; 20.6g protein; 16.9g fibre

3 eggs

¼ teaspoon salt

⅔ cup (100g) plain (all-purpose) flour

1½ cups (375ml) milk

2 tablespoons olive oil

¾ cup (90g) coarsely grated cheddar cheese

MUSHROOM FILLING

20g (¾ ounce) butter

2 tablespoons olive oil

1 medium brown onion (150g), chopped finely

4 cloves garlic, crushed

1 fresh long red chilli, chopped finely

500g (1 pound) button mushrooms, chopped finely

¼ cup finely chopped fresh coriander

CORIANDER SAUCE

1 tablespoon olive oil

1 large brown onion (200g), chopped finely

4 cloves garlic, crushed

1 cup (250ml) pouring cream

½ cup (120g) sour cream

¾ cup finely chopped fresh coriander

½ cup (60g) coarsely grated cheddar cheese

mushroom crêpes with
CORIANDER SAUCE

PREP + COOK TIME 1 HOUR 30 MINUTES **SERVES 6**

1 Whisk eggs, salt, flour, milk and oil in medium bowl until smooth. Cover; stand 30 minutes.

2 Meanwhile, make mushroom filling.

3 Heat oiled heavy-based crêpe pan or small frying pan; pour ¼ cup of batter into pan, tilting pan to coat base. Cook, over low heat, until browned lightly, loosening edge of crêpe with spatula. Turn crêpe; brown other side. Remove crêpe from pan; cover to keep warm. Repeat with remaining batter to make a total of 12 crêpes.

4 Preheat oven to 180°C/350°F.

5 Place heaped tablespoons of filling along centre of each crêpe; roll crêpes to enclose filling. Place crêpes, in single layer, in oiled shallow baking dish; top with cheese.

6 Bake crêpes about 15 minutes or until filling is hot and cheese is browned lightly.

7 Meanwhile, make coriander sauce.

8 Serve crêpes with sauce.

MUSHROOM FILLING Heat butter and oil in large frying pan; cook onion, garlic and chilli, stirring, until onion softens. Add mushrooms; cook, stirring, about 15 minutes or until mushrooms are soft and water has evaporated. Cool slightly; stir in coriander, season to taste.

CORIANDER SAUCE Heat oil in large frying pan; cook onion and garlic, stirring, until onion softens. Add cream; simmer, uncovered, about 10 minutes or until thickened. Remove from heat; stir in sour cream, coriander and cheese. Season to taste.

nutritional count per serving 58g total fat (28.9g saturated fat); 2867kJ (686 cal); 19.1g carbohydrate; 19.1g protein; 4.4g fibre

black bean, corn and
CHIPOTLE STEW

PREP + COOK TIME 1 HOUR 15 MINUTES (+ STANDING) ⚙ SERVES 4

1½ cups (300g) dried black beans

2 chipotle chillies

½ cup (125ml) boiling water

1 tablespoon cumin seeds

2 corn cobs (800g), trimmed

2 teaspoons olive oil

1 large brown onion (200g), chopped finely

800g (1½ pounds) canned crushed tomatoes

8 x 15cm (6-inch) white corn tortillas

SALSA FRESCA

1 small red onion (100g), chopped coarsely

1 small tomato (90g), chopped coarsely

½ cup coarsely chopped fresh coriander

1 lebanese cucumber (130g), chopped coarsely

1 tablespoon olive oil

2 tablespoons lemon juice

1 Place beans in medium bowl, cover with water; stand overnight, drain. Rinse under cold water; drain. Cook beans in medium saucepan of boiling water about 15 minutes or until beans are just tender. Drain.

2 Preheat oven to 200°C/400°F.

3 Cover chillies with the boiling water in small heatproof bowl; stand 20 minutes. Discard stems; blend or process chilli and soaking liquid until smooth.

4 Meanwhile, dry-fry cumin seeds in small frying pan, stirring, until fragrant.

5 Cook corn on heated oiled grill plate (or grill or barbecue) until browned lightly and just tender. When cool enough to handle, cut kernels from cobs.

6 Heat oil in large flameproof dish; cook onion, stirring, until softened. Add drained beans, chilli mixture, cumin, undrained tomatoes and half the corn; bring to the boil. Cook, uncovered, in oven, about 20 minutes or until sauce thickens. Season to taste.

7 Meanwhile, heat tortillas according to instructions on packet. Make salsa fresca.

8 Serve stew with tortillas and salsa.

SALSA FRESCA Combine remaining corn with salsa ingredients in medium bowl; season to taste.

nutritional count per serving 10.4g total fat (1.3g saturated fat); 1839kJ (440 cal); 61.3g carbohydrate; 26.2g protein; 19.5g fibre

TO ADD EXTRA HEAT SERVE SOME PICKLED
SLICED JALAPENO CHILLIES WITH THE TACOS.

1 tablespoon olive oil
1 medium brown onion (150g), chopped finely
500g (1 pound) minced (ground) chicken
35g (1 ounce) packet taco seasoning mix
375g (12 ounces) bottled thick and chunky taco sauce
½ cup (125ml) water
10 stand 'n' stuff taco shells (140g)
1 cup (60g) finely shredded iceberg lettuce
1 medium carrot (120g), grated coarsely
125g (4 ounces) cherry tomatoes, quartered
½ cup (60g) coarsely grated cheddar cheese
½ cup loosely packed fresh coriander leaves
⅓ cup (80g) sour cream

1 Heat oil in large frying pan; cook onion, stirring, until softened. Add chicken; cook, stirring, until browned. Add taco seasoning; cook, stirring, until fragrant. Add half the taco sauce and the water; cook, stirring occasionally, about 7 minutes or until mixture thickens. Remove from heat; season to taste.
2 Meanwhile, heat taco shells according to directions on packet.
3 Divide chicken mixture into shells; top with lettuce, carrot, tomato, cheese, coriander, sour cream and remaining sauce.

nutritional count per taco 35.9g total fat
(13.3g saturated fat); 2445kJ (585 cal);
29.7g carbohydrate; 33.2g protein; 6.7g fibre

spicy
CHICKEN
TACOS

PREP + COOK TIME 25 MINUTES ☼ MAKES 10

snapper VERACRUZ

PREP + COOK TIME 1 HOUR (+ COOLING) ✿ **SERVES 4**

¼ cup (60ml) light olive oil

2 medium green capsicum (bell peppers) (400g),
  chopped coarsely

1 medium brown onion (150g), chopped coarsely

2 fresh small red thai (serrano) chillies, chopped finely

2 cloves garlic, crushed

¼ teaspoon ground white pepper

1 teaspoon ground cinnamon

4 medium tomatoes (600g), chopped coarsely

¾ cup (110g) pimiento-stuffed green olives,
  chopped coarsely

2 tablespoons drained capers, rinsed, chopped coarsely

1 tablespoon lemon juice

2 x 800g (1½-pound) whole snapper

1 Heat oil in large frying pan; cook capsicum,
onion, chilli and garlic, stirring, until onion softens.
Add pepper, cinnamon and tomato; simmer,
uncovered, stirring occasionally, about 10 minutes
or until tomatoes have broken down and sauce
is thick. Stir in olives, capers and juice; season to
taste. Cool.

2 Preheat oven to 180°C/350°F.

3 Score fish three times each side through thickest
part of flesh; place fish in large baking dish, season.
Pour tomato mixture over fish.

4 Bake fish, uncovered, about 30 minutes or until
fish is cooked through. Serve with lemon wedges.

nutritional count per serving 19.7g total fat
(3.5g saturated fat); 1710kJ (409 cal);
8.1g carbohydrate; 46.7g protein; 5.5g fibre

paprika and parmesan polenta
WITH WALNUT AND CAPSICUM SALSA

PREP + COOK TIME 1 HOUR (+ REFRIGERATION)   SERVES 6

YOU CAN USE OLIVE OIL INSTEAD OF
THE WALNUT OIL, IF YOU PREFER.

20g (¾ ounce) butter

2 medium brown onions (300g), sliced thinly

1 tablespoon light brown sugar

1 litre (4 cups) water

1⅓ cups (225g) polenta

2 teaspoons smoked paprika

1 tablespoon red wine vinegar

1 cup (80g) coarsely grated parmesan cheese

WALNUT AND CAPSICUM SALSA

2 large red capsicums (bell peppers) (700g)

1½ cups (150g) roasted walnuts, chopped coarsely

1 tablespoon red wine vinegar

¼ cup (60ml) walnut oil

1 clove garlic, crushed

½ cup coarsely chopped fresh flat-leaf parsley

⅓ cup coarsely chopped fresh coriander

1 Melt butter in medium frying pan; cook onion, stirring, until softened. Add sugar and 2 tablespoons of the water; cook, stirring, about 5 minutes or until onion caramelises. Cover to keep warm.

2 Oil deep 22cm (9-inch) round cake pan. Bring remaining water to the boil in medium saucepan. Gradually add polenta and paprika, stirring constantly. Simmer, stirring, about 8 minutes or until polenta thickens. Stir in vinegar and cheese then spread half the polenta into pan. Spread onion mixture over polenta, spread remaining polenta over onion. Cover; refrigerate 3 hours or until firm.

3 Meanwhile, make walnut and capsicum salsa.

4 Turn polenta onto board; cut into six wedges. Cook polenta, both sides, on heated oiled grill plate (or grill or barbecue) until browned lightly and hot. Serve polenta with salsa.

WALNUT AND CAPSICUM SALSA Preheat grill (broiler). Quarter capsicums, discard seeds and membranes. Place capsicum, skin-side up, on oven tray; grill until skin blisters and blackens. Cover capsicum pieces in plastic or paper for 5 minutes; peel away skin, chop coarsely. Combine capsicum and remaining ingredients in small bowl; season to taste.

nutritional count per serving 51.8g total fat (10.6g saturated fat); 3210kJ (768 cal); 51.9g carbohydrate; 21.2g protein; 7.1g fibre

chicken quesadillas
WITH GUACAMOLE

PREP + COOK TIME 45 MINUTES ✷ **SERVES 4**

1 tablespoon olive oil

1 small red onion (100g), chopped finely

2 cloves garlic, crushed

¼ teaspoon cayenne pepper

2 teaspoons ground cumin

1 medium red capsicum (bell pepper) (200g), chopped finely

1 medium green capsicum (bell pepper) (200g), chopped finely

3 cups (480g) shredded barbecued chicken

8 x 20cm (8-inch) flour tortillas

2 cups (240g) coarsely grated cheddar cheese

⅓ cup loosely packed fresh coriander leaves

GUACAMOLE

2 large avocados (640g), chopped coarsely

½ small red onion (50g), chopped finely

1 large tomato (220g), seeded, chopped finely

2 tablespoons lime juice

1 tablespoon finely chopped fresh coriander

1 Heat oil in large frying pan; cook onion and garlic, stirring, until onion softens. Add spices and capsicums; cook, stirring, until capsicums soften. Remove from heat; stir in chicken. Season to taste.

2 Place one tortilla on board; top with ¼ cup of the cheese, then a quarter of the chicken mixture and another ¼ cup of the cheese. Top with a second tortilla. Repeat with remaining tortillas, cheese and chicken mixture.

3 Cook quesadillas, one at a time, in same oiled pan, over medium heat, until golden brown both sides. Remove from pan; cover to keep warm while cooking remaining quesadillas.

4 Meanwhile, make guacamole.

5 Serve quesadillas, cut into quarters, with guacamole, coriander and, if you like, a dollop of sour cream.

GUACAMOLE Mash avocado in medium bowl; stir in remaining ingredients. Season to taste.

nutritional count per serving 66g total fat (22.7g saturated fat); 4393kJ (1051 cal); 54.3g carbohydrate; 57.1g protein; 6.7g fibre

pork ribs with chorizo and
SMOKED PAPRIKA

PREP + COOK TIME 2 HOURS 15 MINUTES SERVES 4

1.5kg (3 pounds) american-style pork spareribs

4 cloves garlic, crushed

2 teaspoons smoked paprika

1 tablespoon olive oil

1 cured chorizo sausage (170g), sliced thinly

1 tablespoon olive oil, extra

1 medium red onion (170g), chopped coarsely

1 medium red capsicum (bell pepper) (200g), chopped coarsely

1 tablespoon light brown sugar

800g (1½ pounds) canned chopped tomatoes

1 cup (250ml) chicken stock

1 Cut between bones of pork to separate into individual ribs. Combine garlic, paprika and oil in small bowl; rub over pork ribs.

2 Preheat oven to 160°C/325°F.

3 Cook chorizo in heated large flameproof baking dish, stirring, until browned lightly. Remove from dish with slotted spoon; drain on absorbent paper.

4 Cook ribs, in same dish, in batches, until browned. Drain on absorbent paper.

5 Add extra oil, onion and capsicum to same dish; cook, stirring, until onion softens. Return ribs and chorizo to dish with sugar, undrained tomatoes and stock; bring to the boil.

6 Cover dish tightly with foil; cook, in oven, 1 hour. Remove foil; cook further 30 minutes or until ribs are tender. Season to taste.

nutritional count per serving 38.5g total fat (11.4g saturated fat); 2516kJ (602 cal); 15.6g carbohydrate; 49.2g protein; 4.1g fibre

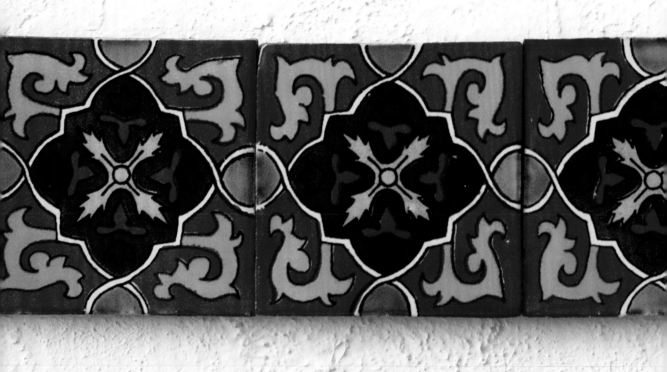

BEANS
AND RICE

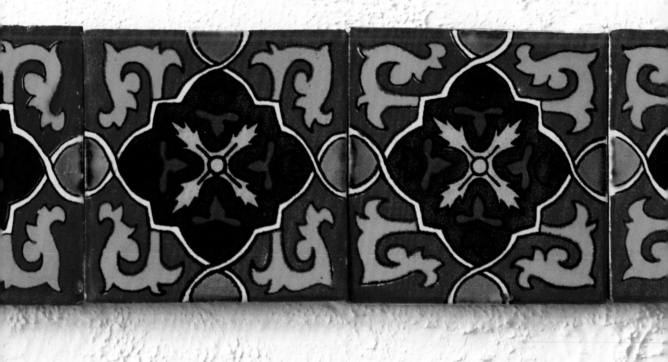

THE STEM OF ZUCCHINI IS THE BABY ZUCCHINI ATTACHED TO THE FLOWER. YOU NEED TO COOK ABOUT 1½ CUPS (300G) WHITE LONG-GRAIN RICE FOR THIS RECIPE. SPREAD COOKED RICE ON A FLAT TRAY AND REFRIGERATE, UNCOVERED, OVERNIGHT BEFORE USING.

saffron rice
WITH ZUCCHINI FLOWERS

PREP + COOK TIME 30 MINUTES ⚙ SERVES 4

12 zucchini (courgette) flowers, stem attached (240g)
45g (1½ ounces) butter
1 large red onion (300g), cut into wedges
2 teaspoons caraway seeds
1 clove garlic, crushed
4 cups (850g) cooked white long-grain rice
1 teaspoon ground turmeric
pinch saffron threads
¼ cup (20g) flaked almonds, roasted

1 Remove flowers from zucchini; discard stamens from flowers. Slice zucchini thinly.
2 Melt butter in large frying pan; cook onion, seeds and garlic, stirring, until onion softens. Add sliced zucchini; cook, stirring, until tender. Add rice, spices and zucchini flowers; cook, stirring, until hot. Stir in half the nuts; season to taste.
3 Serve sprinkled with remaining nuts.

nutritional count per serving 12.9g total fat (6.2g saturated fat); 1747kJ (418 cal); 65.3g carbohydrate; 8g protein; 3.6g fibre

1 medium brown onion (150g), quartered

2 large tomatoes (440g), quartered

2 cloves garlic, unpeeled

2 tablespoons olive oil

½ teaspoon chilli powder

1½ cups (300g) white long-grain rice

2 cups (500ml) chicken stock

1 small carrot (70g), sliced thinly

½ cup (60g) frozen peas

125g (4 ounces) canned corn kernels, drained

⅓ cup coarsely chopped fresh coriander

1 Preheat oven to 200°C/400°F.

2 Place onion, tomato and garlic on oiled oven tray; drizzle with half the oil. Roast, uncovered, about 25 minutes or until vegetables soften. When cool enough to handle, peel tomato and garlic.

3 Blend or process onion, tomato, garlic and chilli powder until smooth; you need 2 cups puree.

4 Heat remaining oil in medium saucepan; cook rice, stirring, 3 minutes. Add tomato mixture; cook, stirring, about 8 minutes or until almost all of the liquid is evaporated. Add stock, carrot, peas and corn; bring to the boil. Reduce heat; simmer, covered, over low heat, about 10 minutes or until rice is tender and liquid is absorbed. Remove from heat; stand, covered, 10 minutes. Fluff rice with a fork; season to taste. Serve sprinkled with coriander.

nutritional count per serving 7.9g total fat (1.2g saturated fat); 1739kJ (416 cal); 72.9g carbohydrate; 10g protein; 5.3g fibre

MEXICAN RICE

PREP + COOK TIME 1 HOUR ⚙ SERVES 4

REFRIED BEANS

PREP + COOK TIME 2 HOURS 30 MINUTES ⚙ **SERVES**

1¾ cups (350g) dried kidney beans
1.5 litres (6 cups) water
1 small brown onion (80g), chopped coarsely
1 clove garlic, crushed
1 dried bay leaf
½ fresh small green chilli, chopped finely
2 tablespoons olive oil
1 small brown onion (80g), chopped finely
1 large tomato (220g), peeled, chopped finely

1 Combine beans, the water, coarsely chopped onion, garlic, bay leaf and chilli in large saucepan; bring to the boil. Reduce heat; simmer, covered, about 1½ hours or until beans are tender.
2 Drain bean mixture, discard bay leaf; reserve ½ cup cooking liquid. Blend or process bean mixture with reserved cooking liquid until coarsely mashed.
3 Heat oil in large frying pan; cook finely chopped onion, stirring, until onion softens. Add tomato; cook, stirring, until tomato softens. Stir in bean mixture; cook, stirring, about 10 minutes or until thickened. Season to taste.

nutritional count per serving 7.2g total fat
(1g saturated fat); 1003kJ (240 cal);
23g carbohydrate; 13.9g protein; 13.4g fibre

SERVING SUGGESTION
Serve as a dip with corn chips or use as a vegetarian filling for tacos, quesadillas or burritos.

red beans
AND RICE

PREP + COOK TIME 1 HOUR ✦ **SERVES 4**

RED BEANS AND RICE IS A FILLING AND BUDGET-FRIENDLY DISH. IF YOU LIKE, SERVE WITH GRILLED CHICKEN FOR A MEATIER MEAL OR IT CAN BE SERVED AS A SIDE DISH TO ACCOMPANY MANY OF THE MAIN MEALS IN THIS BOOK. YOU NEED ONE TRIMMED CORN COB TO GET THE AMOUNT OF CORN KERNELS REQUIRED FOR THIS RECIPE; YOU CAN USE THE SAME AMOUNT OF DRAINED CANNED CORN KERNELS OR FROZEN CORN KERNELS, IF YOU PREFER.

2 rindless bacon slices (130g), chopped coarsely
1 medium brown onion (150g), chopped finely
1 small red capsicum (bell pepper) (150g), chopped finely
2 cloves garlic, crushed
1 tablespoon tomato purée
1 tablespoon red wine vinegar
1 teaspoon smoked paprika
2 cups (400g) white long-grain rice
1 dried bay leaf
1 cup (250ml) chicken stock
2¼ cups (560ml) water
410g (13 ounces) canned kidney beans, drained, rinsed
½ cup (80g) corn kernels
1 tablespoon lime juice

1 Cook bacon in heated large frying pan, stirring, until starting to crisp. Add onion, capsicum and garlic; cook, stirring until onion softens.
2 Add paste, vinegar and paprika; cook, stirring, 1 minute. Add rice; cook, stirring, 2 minutes.
3 Add bay leaf, stock, the water and beans; bring to the boil. Reduce heat; simmer, covered, 20 minutes. Add corn; cook, covered, about 5 minutes or until rice is tender. Remove from heat; stand, covered, 5 minutes. Stir in juice; season to taste.

nutritional count per serving 3.3g total fat (1g saturated fat); 2215kJ (530 cal); 99.3g carbohydrate; 20.8g protein; 7.1g fibre

1 large green capsicum (bell pepper) (350g)

2 medium brown onions (300g), quartered

4 cloves garlic, unpeeled

2 fresh small green chillies

¼ cup (60ml) olive oil

3 cups (750ml) chicken stock

⅓ cup each firmly packed fresh flat-leaf parsley
leaves and coriander (cilantro) leaves

1½ cups (300g) white long-grain rice

1 Preheat oven to 200°C/400°F.

2 Quarter capsicum; discard seeds and membranes. Place capsicum, onion, garlic and chilli on oiled oven tray; drizzle with 1 tablespoon oil. Roast, uncovered, about 25 minutes or until vegetables soften. When cool enough to handle, peel capsicum and garlic; discard stems from chillies.

3 Blend or process capsicum, onion, garlic and chilli with 1 cup stock until combined. Add herbs; blend or process until smooth.

4 Heat remaining oil in medium saucepan; cook rice, stirring, about 3 minutes or until rice is browned lightly. Stir in herb mixture and remaining stock; bring to the boil. Reduce heat; simmer, covered, about 15 minutes or until rice is tender and liquid is absorbed. Remove from heat; stand, covered, 10 minutes. Fluff rice with a fork; season to taste.

nutritional count per serving 14.4g total fat (2.2g saturated fat); 1839kJ (440 cal); 67.3g carbohydrate; 9g protein; 2.7g fibre

GREEN RICE

PREP + COOK TIME 50 MINUTES ✸ SERVES 4

DRUNKEN BEANS

PREP + COOK TIME 1 HOUR 50 MINUTES (+ STANDING) SERVES 4

1 cup (200g) dried pinto beans

3 rindless bacon slices (195g), chopped coarsely

1 medium brown onion (150g), chopped finely

1 clove garlic, crushed

1 teaspoon ground cumin

½ teaspoon cayenne pepper

1 tablespoon tomato paste

400g (12½ ounces) canned crushed tomatoes

1 cup (250ml) water

1 cup (250ml) beer

1 tablespoon worcestershire sauce

2 tablespoons light brown sugar

1 Place beans in medium bowl, cover with water; stand overnight. Drain.

2 Cook bacon, onion, garlic and spices in oiled large saucepan, stirring, until onion softens.

3 Add drained beans and remaining ingredients to pan; bring to the boil. Reduce heat; simmer, covered, about 1½ hours or until beans are just tender. Season to taste.

nutritional count per serving 4.8g total fat (1.5g saturated fat); 1267kJ (303 cal); 32.1g carbohydrate; 21.6g protein; 12.8g fibre

SALSAS AND SAUCES

HOT SAUCE IS THE PERFECT CONDIMENT TO USE IF YOU WANT TO ADD EXTRA SPICE TO YOUR MEAL. SPOON A LITTLE HOT SAUCE ON ENCHILADAS, TACOS OR EVEN SCRAMBLED EGGS, IF YOU LIKE.

3 ancho chillies
1 cup (250ml) boiling water
6 medium ripe tomatoes (900g), chopped coarsely
4 cloves garlic, quartered
1 small brown onion (80g), chopped coarsely
3 cloves
2 tablespoons red wine vinegar
1 teaspoon dried thyme leaves
½ teaspoon dried oregano leaves
½ teaspoon ground cumin
2 tablespoons olive oil

1   Cover chillies with the boiling water in small heatproof bowl; stand 20 minutes.
2   Meanwhile, blend or process tomato until smooth.
3   Discard stalks from chillies; blend or process chilli and soaking liquid with garlic, onion, cloves, vinegar, herbs and cumin until smooth.
4   Heat oil in large frying pan; cook chilli mixture, stirring, until mixture comes to the boil. Add tomato mixture; simmer, uncovered, stirring occasionally, about 1 hour or until reduced to about 3 cups. Season to taste; cool.

nutritional count per ¼ cup 3.1g total fat (0.4g saturated fat); 176kJ (42 cal); 1.9g carbohydrate; 0.9g protein; 1.2g fibre

HOT SAUCE

PREP + COOK TIME 1 HOUR 30 MINUTES ✹ MAKES 3 CUPS

mango and
AVOCADO SALSA

PREP TIME 15 MINUTES ✦ **MAKES 2½ CUPS**

1 medium mango (430g), chopped coarsely

1 large avocado (320g), chopped coarsely

1 small red onion (100g), chopped finely

1 small red capsicum (bell pepper) (150g),
chopped finely

1 fresh small red thai (serrano) chilli, chopped finely

2 tablespoons lime juice

1 Combine ingredients in medium bowl;
season to taste.

nutritional count per tablespoon 1.7g total fat
(0.4g saturated fat); 100kJ (24 cal);
1.6g carbohydrate; 0.4g protein; 0.4g fibre

SERVING SUGGESTION
Serve with roasted corn, grilled chicken
or salmon fillets.

SERVING SUGGESTION
Serve with grilled salmon or chicken,
barbecued rump steak, beef or chicken fajitas;
this recipe makes enough for six servings.

grilled corn and
ZUCCHINI SALSA

PREP + COOK TIME 30 MINUTES ⚙ **MAKES 7 CUPS**

2 trimmed corn cobs (500g)

100g (3 ounces) baby zucchini (courgette),
   halved lengthways

2 large avocados (640g), chopped coarsely

200g (6½ ounces) grape tomatoes, halved

1 medium red onion (170g), sliced thickly

¼ cup coarsely chopped fresh coriander

1 tablespoon sweet chilli sauce

⅓ cup (80ml) lime juice

2 fresh small red thai (serrano) chillies, sliced thinly

1 Cook corn and zucchini on heated oiled grill
plate (or grill or barbecue) until tender and
browned lightly. When cool enough to handle,
remove kernels from cobs.

2 Place corn and zucchini in large bowl with
avocado, tomato, onion and coriander. Add
combined sauce, juice and chilli; toss gently
to combine. Season to taste.

nutritional count per tablespoon 1.3g total fat
(0.3g saturated fat); 84kJ (20 cal);
1.4g carbohydrate; 0.5g protein; 0.5g fibre

black bean and
MANGO SALSA

PREP + COOK TIME 1 HOUR 40 MINUTES (+ STANDING) ⚙ SERVES 6

1 cup (200g) dried black beans
1 lebanese cucumber (130g), seeded, sliced thinly
1 medium mango (430g), chopped finely
1 cup loosely packed fresh coriander leaves

SWEET CHILLI DRESSING

1 tablespoon olive oil
1 tablespoon sweet chilli sauce
1 tablespoon lime juice

1 Place beans in medium bowl, cover with water; stand overnight. Drain.
2 Cook beans in medium saucepan of boiling water until tender; drain.
3 Meanwhile, make sweet chilli dressing.
4 Place beans in medium bowl with dressing and remaining ingredients; toss gently to combine, season to taste.

SWEET CHILLI DRESSING Combine ingredients in small bowl.

nutritional count per serving 9.9g total fat (1.5g saturated fat); 790kJ (189 cal); 9.7g carbohydrate; 11.6g protein; 7.8g fibre

2 medium avocados (500g)

½ small red onion (50g), chopped finely

1 medium egg (plum) tomato (75g), seeded, chopped finely

1 tablespoon lime juice

¼ cup coarsely chopped fresh coriander

1 Mash avocados in medium bowl; stir in remaining ingredients. Season to taste.

nutritional count per tablespoon 2.6g total fat (0.6g saturated fat); 109kJ (26 cal); 0.2g carbohydrate; 0.3g protein; 0.2g fibre

SERVING SUGGESTION

Serve as a dip with corn chips; it also goes well with nachos, burritos and fajitas.

GUACAMOLE

PREP TIME 10 MINUTES ✸ MAKES 2½ CUPS

SWEET TREATS

FLAN DE CAFE

PREP + COOK TIME 50 MINUTES (+ REFRIGERATION) ⚙ MAKES 6

¾ cup (165g) caster sugar
¾ cup (180ml) water
6 eggs
⅓ cup (75g) caster sugar, extra
2 tablespoons coffee-flavoured liqueur
1 tablespoon instant coffee granules
1 tablespoon water, extra
1½ cups (375ml) milk
1¼ cups (310ml) thickened (heavy) cream

1 Preheat oven to 160°C/325°F.
2 Stir sugar and the water in medium saucepan over heat, without boiling, until sugar dissolves. Bring to the boil; boil, uncovered, without stirring, about 5 minutes or until mixture is golden brown. Pour evenly into six 1-cup (250ml) ovenproof dishes.
3 Whisk eggs and extra sugar together in medium bowl; stir in liqueur and combined coffee and the extra water.

4 Bring milk and cream to the boil in medium saucepan. Remove from heat; allow bubbles to subside. Gradually whisk milk mixture into egg mixture; strain into jug.
5 Place dishes in baking dish; pour custard into dishes. Pour enough boiling water into baking dish to come halfway up sides of dishes.
6 Bake flans about 30 minutes or until just set. Remove dishes from water; cool to room temperature. Refrigerate overnight.
7 Turn flans onto serving plates, serve with extra whipped cream and orange rind, if you like.

nutritional count per flan 26.9g total fat (15.9g saturated fat); 1363kJ (326 cal); 48.1g carbohydrate; 10g protein; 0.1g fibre

IT IS FINE TO USE JUST ONE 300ml CARTON OF CREAM FOR THIS RECIPE.

grilled bananas with
COCONUT SYRUP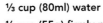

PREP + COOK TIME 15 MINUTES ⚙ SERVES 4

⅓ cup (80ml) water
¼ cup (55g) firmly packed light brown sugar
¼ cup (60ml) coconut-flavoured liqueur
4 large ripe bananas (920g)
2 teaspoons finely grated lime rind
¼ cup (20g) shredded coconut, toasted

1 Stir the water and sugar in small saucepan over heat, without boiling, until sugar dissolves; bring to the boil. Reduce heat; simmer, uncovered, without stirring, about 3 minutes or until syrup thickens slightly. Remove from heat; stir in liqueur.
2 Split bananas lengthways; brush about a quarter of the syrup mixture over the cut-sides of bananas.
3 Cook bananas, cut-side down, on heated lightly oiled grill plate (or grill or barbecue) until browned lightly and heated through.
4 Meanwhile, heat remaining syrup mixture in small saucepan until hot. Remove from heat; stir in rind.
5 Serve hot bananas drizzled with syrup; sprinkle with coconut.

nutritional count per serving 3.5g total fat (2.6g saturated fat); 1116kJ (267 cal); 47g carbohydrate; 2.6g protein; 3.7g fibre

WE USED MALIBU, A RUM-BASED COCONUT LIQUEUR, FOR THIS RECIPE.

SERVING SUGGESTION
Serve with whipped cream or ice-cream.

4 eggs
¼ cup (55g) caster sugar
1¾ cups (260g) plain (all-purpose) flour
½ cup (75g) self-raising flour
½ teaspoon salt
vegetable oil, for shallow-frying
1¼ cups (275g) caster sugar, extra
1½ teaspoons ground cinnamon

1 Beat eggs and sugar in small bowl with electric mixer until thick and creamy. Transfer mixture to large bowl; stir in sifted flours and salt, in two batches. Knead dough on floured surface until smooth and no longer sticky. Wrap in plastic; stand 20 minutes.
2 Divide dough into 16 portions. Roll each portion on floured surface into 12cm (4¾-inch) rounds.
3 Heat oil in large frying pan; shallow-fry pastries, one at a time, turning once, until browned lightly. Drain on absorbent paper.
4 Toss hot pastries in combined extra sugar and cinnamon. Serve warm or cold.

nutritional count per pastry 5.9g total fat (1g saturated fat); 548kJ (131 cal); 32.2g carbohydrate; 3.9g protein; 0.8g fibre

fried SWEET PASTRIES

PREP + COOK TIME 45 MINUTES (+ STANDING) ⚙ MAKES 16

ROYAL EGGS

PREP + COOK TIME 50 MINUTES (+ STANDING) ✸ SERVES 4

12 egg yolks
2 teaspoons baking powder
1 teaspoon water
1 teaspoon melted butter

CINNAMON SYRUP

2 cups (440g) caster sugar
1 cup (250ml) water
3 cinnamon sticks, broken
½ cup (125ml) dry sherry
2 tablespoons lime juice
⅓ cup (50g) raisins
⅓ cup (50g) pine nuts, roasted

1 Preheat oven to 160°C/325°F. Grease deep 20cm (8-inch) square cake pan; line base with baking paper, grease paper.
2 Beat egg yolks and baking powder in small bowl with electric mixer until thick and creamy; fold in the water and butter. Pour mixture into pan.
3 Place pan in baking dish; add enough boiling water to dish to come half way up sides of pan.
4 Bake cake about 15 minutes or until firm. Remove pan from water; stand 10 minutes.
5 Meanwhile, make cinnamon syrup.
6 Carefully turn cake onto board; cut into squares. Place squares in deep heatproof dish, pour over hot syrup; stand until syrup is cool.

CINNAMON SYRUP Stir sugar, the water, cinnamon, sherry and juice in medium saucepan, over heat, without boiling, until sugar dissolves; bring to the boil. Reduce heat; simmer, uncovered, without stirring, about 3 minutes or until thickened slightly. Remove from heat; stir in raisins and nuts.

nutritional count per serving 26.8g total fat (7g saturated fat); 1488kJ (356 cal); 120g carbohydrate; 11.4g protein; 1.3g fibre

coconut and pineapple
CHIMICHANGAS

PREP + COOK TIME 45 MINUTES ✷ **MAKES 16**

⅔ cup (180g) canned crushed pineapple, drained
½ cup (85g) finely chopped raisins
⅓ cup (110g) apricot jam
2 teaspoons ground cinnamon
½ cup (40g) shredded coconut
8 x 15cm (6-inch) flour tortillas
vegetable oil, for deep-frying
1 tablespoon icing sugar

1 Combine pineapple, raisins, jam, cinnamon and coconut in medium bowl.
2 Heat tortillas according to instructions on packet.
3 Divide pineapple mixture evenly between tortillas. Roll tortillas up firmly, folding in sides; secure with toothpicks.
4 Heat oil in wok or large frying pan; deep-fry tortilla rolls, in batches, until browned lightly. Drain on absorbent paper. Remove toothpicks.
5 Dust chimichangas with sifted icing sugar. Cut each chimichanga in half; serve with ice-cream or whipped cream, if you like.

nutritional count per chimichanga 4.1g total fat (1.7g saturated fat); 427kJ (102 cal); 14.9g carbohydrate; 1.2g protein; 1.4g fibre

mexican
WEDDING COOKIES

PREP + COOK TIME 55 MINUTES (+ REFRIGERATION) ✸ **MAKES 34**

250g (8 ounces) butter, softened
¾ cup (165g) caster sugar
2 cups (300g) plain (all-purpose) flour
½ cup (75g) finely chopped blanched almonds
½ cup (60g) finely chopped pecans
1 tablespoon finely grated orange rind
1 teaspoon vanilla extract
1 egg yolk
¼ cup (40g) icing sugar

1 Preheat oven to 180°C/350°F. Line oven trays with baking paper.
2 Beat butter and caster sugar in small bowl with electric mixer until light and fluffy. Stir in sifted flour, nuts, rind, extract and egg yolk.
3 Shape level tablespoons of dough into rectangles; place biscuits, about 2.5cm (1-inch) apart, on trays. Cover; refrigerate 30 minutes.
4 Bake biscuits about 25 minutes. Stand on trays 5 minutes, before transferring to wire racks to cool. Dust with sifted icing sugar.

nutritional count per cookie 8.8g total fat (4.2g saturated fat); 489kJ (117 cal); 12.7g carbohydrate; 1.7g protein; 0.7g fibre

1 lime

1½ cups (330g) caster sugar

1 cinnamon stick

6 cloves

2½ cups (625ml) water

4 medium pink guavas (720g)

½ teaspoon vanilla extract

1 Using vegetable peeler, peel rind thinly from lime; cut rind into thin strips. Squeeze 1 tablespoon juice from lime.

2 Combine rind, juice, sugar, cinnamon, cloves and the water in medium saucepan; stir over heat, without boiling, until sugar dissolves. Simmer, covered, 20 minutes.

3 Peel guavas; cut into quarters, discard seeds.

4 Add guavas to syrup; simmer, covered loosely, about 10 minutes, or until guavas are tender. Cool guavas in syrup.

5 Remove guavas from syrup; place in medium heatproof bowl. Strain syrup through fine sieve; discard cinnamon and cloves.

6 Return syrup to same pan; simmer, uncovered, about 10 minutes or until reduced to about 1¼ cups. Remove pan from heat; stir in extract. Pour syrup over guavas; cool. Cover; refrigerate.

7 Serve guavas and syrup, if you like, with yogurt, whipped cream or ice-cream.

nutritional count per serving 0.5g total fat (0.1g saturated fat); 142kJ (34 cal); 3.4g carbohydrate; 0.7g protein; 5.1g fibre

poached guavas
IN SPICY SYRUP

PREP + COOK TIME 1 HOUR (+ COOLING) ✳ SERVES 4

THREE KINGS BREAD

PREP + COOK TIME 1 HOUR (+ STANDING) SERVES 12

ON JANUARY 6, THIS FRUIT STUDDED BREAD, COMMONLY KNOWN AS THE ROUND BREAD OF THE KINGS, CELEBRATES THE OCCASION WHEN THE THREE KINGS VISITED JESUS.

1 tablespoon (14g) dried yeast

1 teaspoon caster sugar

¼ cup (60ml) warm water

2½ cups (375g) plain (all-purpose) flour

1 teaspoon salt

100g (3 ounces) butter, chopped finely

¼ cup (55g) caster sugar, extra

2 teaspoons each finely grated orange and lemon rind

2 eggs, beaten lightly

4 egg yolks

¼ cup (60g) coarsely chopped glacé figs

¼ cup (60g) coarsely chopped glacé apricots

¼ cup (40g) coarsely chopped raisins

¼ cup (25g) coarsely chopped roasted walnuts

1 egg, beaten lightly, extra

1 slice (40g) glacé orange, chopped coarsely

1 tablespoon coarsely chopped roasted walnuts, extra

ORANGE ICING

1¼ cups (200g) icing (confectioners') sugar

2 tablespoons orange juice

1 Combine yeast, sugar and the water in small bowl. Cover; stand in warm place about 10 minutes or until mixture is frothy.

2 Sift flour and salt into large bowl; rub in butter. Stir in extra sugar and rind. Combine yeast mixture, eggs and egg yolks in medium bowl; stir into flour mixture, mix to a soft dough.

3 Knead dough on floured surface about 10 minutes or until smooth and elastic. Place dough in large oiled bowl. Cover; stand in warm place about 1 hour or until dough doubles in size.

4 Toss figs, apricots, raisins and nuts in about 1 tablespoon of plain flour, breaking up any chunks of fruit. Turn dough onto floured surface, add fruit and nut mixture; knead until smooth.

5 Roll dough into 48cm (19¼-inch) log; shape log into ring, press ends together firmly. Place ring on greased oven tray around a greased 9cm (3¾-inch) ovenproof dish so the ring stays in shape during cooking. Cover; stand in warm place about 50 minutes or until doubled in size.

6 Preheat oven to 200°C/400°F.

7 Brush ring with extra egg; bake 10 minutes. Reduce oven to 180°C/350°F. Bake bread about 15 minutes. Place bread on wire rack over tray, stand 30 minutes.

8 Make orange icing.

9 Pour icing over bread; decorate with glacé orange and sprinkle with extra nuts.

ORANGE ICING Combine sifted icing sugar and juice in small jug.

nutritional count per serving 12.5g total fat (5.7g saturated fat); 1430kJ (342 cal); 55.1g carbohydrate; 7.3g protein; 2.4g fibre

1 tablespoon caster sugar
90g (3 ounces) butter, chopped coarsely
1 cup (150g) plain (all-purpose) flour
2 eggs
vegetable oil, for deep-frying

ANISEED SUGAR

5 star anise
½ cup (110g) caster sugar

1 Make aniseed sugar.
2 Bring the water, sugar and butter to the boil in medium saucepan. Add sifted flour; beat with wooden spoon over high heat until mixture comes away from base and side of pan to form a smooth ball. Transfer mixture to small bowl; beat in eggs, one at a time, with electric mixer until mixture becomes glossy.
3 Spoon mixture into piping bag fitted with a 1cm (½-inch) fluted tube.
4 Heat oil in large saucepan; pipe 6cm (2¼-inch) lengths of batter into oil (cut off lengths with a knife). Deep-fry churros, in batches, about 6 minutes or until browned lightly and crisp. Drain on absorbent paper.
5 Roll churros in aniseed sugar. Serve warm.

ANISEED SUGAR Blend or process ingredients until ground finely.

nutritional count per churro 3.4g total fat (1.6g saturated fat); 247kJ (59 cal); 6.8g carbohydrate; 0.9g protein; 0.2g fibre

CHURROS

PREP + COOK TIME 30 MINUTES ⚙ **MAKES 35**
1 cup (250ml) water

strawberry and peach
TEQUILA POPSICLES

PREP TIME 30 MINUTES (+ FREEZING) MAKES 12

3 medium peaches (450g), chopped coarsely
¼ cup (65g) grated palm sugar
⅓ cup (80ml) tequila
1 tablespoon cointreau
1 tablespoon lemon juice
500g (1 pound) strawberries, chopped coarsely

1 Blend or process peaches until smooth.
Push peaches through a sieve into medium bowl;
stir in half the sugar, half the tequila, cointreau
and juice.
2 Divide half the peach mixture into 12 x ⅓ cup
(80ml) paddle pop moulds (or paper cups);
reserve remaining peach mixture. Freeze about
30 minutes or until surface is firm.
3 Meanwhile, blend or process strawberries until
smooth. Push strawberries through a sieve into
medium bowl; stir in remaining sugar and tequila.
4 Press paddle pop stick firmly into each
popsicle. Divide half the strawberry mixture into
moulds; reserve remaining strawberry mixture.
Freeze about 30 minutes or until surface is firm.
5 Divide remaining peach mixture into moulds;
freeze about 30 minutes or until surface is firm.
6 Divide remaining strawberry mixture into
moulds; freeze popsicles overnight.

nutritional count per popsicle 0.1g total fat
(0g saturated fat); 322kJ (77 cal);
12.5g carbohydrate; 1g protein; 1.4g fibre

GLOSSARY

ALLSPICE also called jamaican pepper or pimento; tastes like a combination of nutmeg, cumin, clove and cinnamon. Sold whole or ground.

ALMONDS
blanched brown skins removed.
flaked paper-thin slices.
slivered small pieces cut lengthways.

BAKING PAPER also called parchment paper or baking parchment; a silicone-coated paper used to line baking pans and oven trays so cakes and biscuits won't stick, making removal easy.

BAKING POWDER a raising agent consisting mainly of two parts cream of tartar to one part bicarbonate of soda. Also available gluten free.

BAY LEAVES aromatic leaves from the bay tree available fresh or dried; adds a strong, slightly peppery flavour.

BEANS
black also called turtle beans or black kidney beans; an earthy-flavoured dried bean completely different from the better-known Chinese black beans (fermented soybeans). Used mostly in Mexican and South American cooking.
borlotti also called roman or pink beans, can be eaten fresh or dried. Interchangeable with pinto beans due to their similarity in appearance – pale pink or beige with dark red streaks.
kidney medium-sized red bean, slightly floury in texture yet sweet in flavour; sold dried or canned, it's often found in bean mixes.
mexican-style a canned mixture of either kidney or pinto beans cooked with tomato, peppers, onion, garlic and various spices.
pinto similar to borlotti, a plump, kidney-shaped, beige bean speckled with brown.
refried pinto beans, cooked twice – soaked and boiled, then mashed and fried, traditionally in lard. A Mexican staple, frijoles refritos or refried beans are available canned in supermarkets.

BLOOD ORANGE a virtually seedless citrus fruit with blood-red-streaked rind and flesh; sweet, non-acidic, salmon-coloured pulp and juice with slight strawberry or raspberry overtones. The rind is not as bitter as an ordinary orange.

BREADCRUMBS
fresh bread, usually white, processed into crumbs.
packaged prepared fine-textured but crunchy white breadcrumbs; good for coating foods that are to be fried.
stale crumbs made by grating or processing one- or two-day-old bread.

BUTTER we use salted butter unless stated otherwise; 125g is equal to 1 stick (4 ounces).

BUTTERMILK originally the term given to the slightly sour liquid left after butter was churned from cream, today it is made from no-fat or low-fat milk to which specific bacterial cultures have been added. Despite its name, it is actually low in fat.

CAPERS the grey-green buds of a warm climate (usually Mediterranean) shrub, sold either dried and salted or pickled in a vinegar brine. Capers should be rinsed before using.

CAPSICUM (BELL PEPPER) also called pepper. Discard seeds and membranes before use.

CARAWAY SEEDS small dried seed from a member of the parsley family; has a sharp anise flavour.

CAYENNE PEPPER a thin-fleshed, long, extremely hot dried red chilli, usually purchased ground.

CHEESE
cheddar semi-hard, yellow to off-white, sharp-tasting cheese.
cream commonly called philadelphia or philly; a soft cow's-milk cheese, its fat content ranges from 14 to 33%.
goat's made from goat's milk, has an earthy, strong taste. Available in soft, crumbly and firm textures, in various shapes and sizes, and sometimes rolled in ash or herbs.
parmesan also known as parmigiano, parmesan is a hard, grainy cow's-milk cheese that originated in the Parma region of Italy. The curd is salted in brine for a month before being aged up to two years in humid conditions.

CHICKEN
breast fillet breast halved, skinned and boned.
drumstick leg with skin and bone intact.
thigh cutlet thigh with skin and centre bone intact; sometimes found skinned with bone intact.

CHILLI
ancho mild, dried chillies commonly

used in Mexican cooking.

chipotle pronounced cheh-pote-lay. The name used for jalapeño chillies once they've been dried and smoked. Having a deep, intensely smoky flavour, rather than a searing heat, chipotles are dark brown, almost black in colour and wrinkled in appearance.

jalapeño pronounced hah-lah-pain-yo. Fairly hot, medium-sized, plump,
dark green chilli; available pickled, sold canned or bottled, and fresh, from greengrocers.

long red available both fresh and dried; a generic term used for any moderately hot, long, thin chilli (about 6cm to 8cm long).

pasilla medium hot, dried chillies; could substitute ground chilli powder.

red thai (serrano) also called "scuds"; tiny, very hot and bright red.

CHOCOLATE, DARK EATING (SEMI-SWEET) also known as semi-sweet or luxury chocolate; made of a high percentage of cocoa liquor and cocoa butter, and little added sugar. Unless stated otherwise, we use dark eating chocolate in this book as it's ideal for use in desserts and cakes.

CHORIZO sausage of Spanish origin, made of coarsely ground pork and highly seasoned with garlic and chilli. They are deeply smoked, very spicy and dry-cured so that they do not need cooking. Also available raw (fresh).

CINNAMON available both in the piece (called sticks or quills) and ground into powder; one of the world's most common spices.

CLOVES dried flower buds of a tropical tree; can be used whole or in ground form. They have a strong scent and taste so should be used sparingly.

COCONUT, SHREDDED unsweetened thin strips of dried coconut flesh.

CORIANDER (CILANTRO) also called pak chee or chinese parsley; bright-green-leafed herb with both pungent aroma and taste. Coriander seeds are dried and sold either whole or ground, and neither tastes remotely like the fresh leaf, so should not be substituted.

CORNFLOUR (CORNSTARCH) made from wheat or 100% corn (maize).

COS (ROMAINE) LETTUCE the traditional caesar salad lettuce. Long, with leaves ranging from dark green on the outside to almost white near the core; the leaves have a stiff centre rib giving a slight cupping effect to the leaf on either side.

CREAM

pouring also called fresh or pure cream; contains no additives and has a minimum fat content 35%.

sour a thick, commercially cultured sour cream with a minimum fat content of 35%.

thick (double) a dolloping cream with a minimum fat content of 45%.

thickened (heavy) a whipping cream containing a thickener. Minimum fat content 35%.

CUCUMBER, LEBANESE short, slender and thin-skinned cucumber. Probably the most popular variety because of its tender, edible skin, tiny, yielding seeds, and sweet, fresh and flavoursome taste.

CUMIN also called zeera or comino; resembling caraway in size, cumin is the dried seed of a plant related to the parsley family. Its spicy, almost curry-like flavour is essential to the traditional foods of Mexico, India, North Africa and the Middle East. Also available ground.

EGGS we use large (60g) chicken eggs unless stated otherwise. If a recipe calls for raw or barely cooked eggs, exercise caution if there is a salmonella problem in your area, particularly in food eaten by children and pregnant women.

FLOUR

plain (all-purpose) unbleached wheat flour, making it the best for baking: the gluten content ensures a strong dough, producing a light result.

self-raising all-purpose plain or wholemeal flour with baking powder and salt added; make at home in the proportion of 1 cup flour to 2 teaspoons baking powder.

GUAVA a round or pear-shaped tropical fruit varying in size. It is thin-skinned with aromatic, sharp-sweet flesh. Varieties include strawberry guava, which is red and tastes of passionfruit and strawberries, and cherry guava which is walnut-size. Guavas are eaten fresh and used for creamy desserts, a jelly preserve and a stiff paste to serve with cheese. Available fresh and canned.

LIQUEUR/SPIRITS

coconut-flavoured we use Malibu.

orange-flavoured we use Cointreau.

tequila colourless alcoholic liquor of Mexican origin made from the fermented sap of the agave, a succulent desert plant.

MUSTARD, DIJON also called french mustard. A pale brown, creamy, fairly mild mustard.

NUTMEG a strong and pungent spice. Usually available ground but the flavour is more intense from a whole nut (from spice shops), so it's best to grate your own. Often included in mixed spice mixtures.

OIL

olive made from ripened olives. Extra virgin and virgin are the first and second press, respectively, of the olives and are therefore considered the best; the "extra light" or "light" name on other types refers to taste not fat levels.

peanut pressed from ground peanuts; the most commonly used oil in Asian cooking because of its high smoke point (capacity to handle high heat without burning).

vegetable oils sourced from plant

rather than animal fats.

ONION
green (scallions) also called, incorrectly, shallot; an immature onion picked before the bulb has formed, with a long, bright-green edible stalk.
red also known as spanish, red spanish or bermuda onion; a sweet-flavoured, large, purple-red onion.

PAPRIKA ground dried sweet red capsicum (bell pepper); many grades and types are available, including sweet, hot, mild and smoked.

PINE NUTS also known as pignoli; not a nut but a small, cream-coloured kernel from pine cones. Best roasted before use to bring out the flavour.

POLENTA also known as cornmeal; a flour-like cereal made of dried corn (maize). Also the dish made from it.

POMEGRANATE Dark-red, leathery-skinned fresh fruit about the size of an orange. The individual cells contain seed kernels that are surrounded by an edible juice-filled sac (pulp).

RAISINS dried sweet grapes (traditionally muscatel grapes).

ROASTING/TOASTING nuts and dried coconut can be roasted in the oven to restore their fresh flavour and release aromatic oils; spread evenly onto an oven tray, roast in a moderate oven about 5 minutes. Desiccated coconut, pine nuts and sesame seeds roast more evenly if stirred over low heat in a heavy-based frying pan; their natural oils help them turn golden.

SAFFRON available in strands or ground; imparts a yellow-orange colour to food once infused. Quality varies greatly; the best is the most expensive spice in the world. Store in the freezer.

SASHIMI fish sold as sashimi has to meet stringent guidelines regarding its handling. We suggest you seek local advice from authorities before eating any raw seafood.

SILVER BEET (SWISS CHARD) also known, incorrectly, as spinach; has fleshy stalks and large leaves, both of which can be prepared as for spinach.

SPINACH also known as english spinach. Baby spinach leaves are best eaten raw in salads; the larger leaves should be added last to dishes, and should be cooked until barely wilted.

STAR ANISE a dried star-shaped pod whose seeds have an astringent aniseed flavour; commonly used to flavour stocks and marinades.

SUGAR
caster (superfine) finely granulated table sugar.
dark brown a moist, dark brown sugar with a rich, distinctive, full flavour coming from natural molasses syrup.
light brown a very soft, finely granulated sugar retaining molasses for its characteristic colour and flavour.
palm also called nam tan pip, jaggery, jawa or gula melaka; made from the sap of the sugar palm tree. Light brown to black in colour and usually sold in rock-hard cakes; substitute with brown sugar.
raw natural brown granulated sugar.

TACO SEASONING MIX packaged seasoning meant to duplicate the mild Mexican sauce made from oregano, cumin, chillies and other spices.

TOMATILLO also called a Mexican green or husk tomato. The fruit looks like a small green tomato covered in a papery husk; it has a thin, bright green skin and a tart, lemony-herb flavour. Tomatillos can ripen to yellow but are generally used while still green and quite firm.

TOMATOES
bottled pasta sauce a prepared tomato-based sauce (sometimes called ragu or sugo on the label); comes in varying degrees of thickness and levels of spicing.
canned whole peeled tomatoes in natural juices; available crushed, chopped or diced. Use undrained.
egg (plum) also called roma; smallish, oval-shaped tomatoes.
paste triple-concentrated tomato puree.

TORTILLA thin, round unleavened bread originating in Mexico; available frozen, fresh or vacuum-packed. Two kinds of tortilla are available, one made from wheat flour and the other from corn.

TURMERIC also called kamin; is a rhizome related to galangal and ginger. Must be grated or pounded to release its acrid aroma and pungent flavour; known for the golden colour it imparts. Ground turmeric can be substituted for the less common fresh turmeric (use 2 teaspoons of ground turmeric plus a teaspoon of sugar for every 20g of fresh turmeric called for in a recipe).

VANILLA EXTRACT made by extracting the flavour from the vanilla bean pod; pods are soaked, usually in alcohol, to capture the authentic flavour.

WATERCRESS a slightly peppery, dark-green leafy vegetable. Highly perishable, so must be used as soon as possible after purchase.

WORCESTERSHIRE SAUCE a dark coloured thin condiment made from garlic, soy sauce, tamarind, onions, molasses, lime, anchovies, vinegar and seasonings. Available in supermarkets.

ZUCCHINI also known as courgette; small, pale- or dark-green, yellow or white vegetable belonging to the squash family. Harvested when young, its edible flowers can be stuffed with a then deep-fried or oven-baked.

CONVERSION CHART

MEASURES

One Australian metric measuring cup holds approximately 250ml; one Australian metric tablespoon holds 20ml; one Australian metric teaspoon holds 5ml.

The difference between one country's measuring cups and another's is within a two- or three-teaspoon variance, and will not affect your cooking results. North America, New Zealand and the United Kingdom use a 15ml tablespoon.

All cup and spoon measurements are level. The most accurate way of measuring dry ingredients is to weigh them. When measuring liquids, use a clear glass or plastic jug with the metric markings.

We use large eggs with an average weight of 60g.

DRY MEASURES

METRIC	IMPERIAL
15g	½oz
30g	1oz
60g	2oz
90g	3oz
125g	4oz (¼lb)
155g	5oz
185g	6oz
220g	7oz
250g	8oz (½lb)
280g	9oz
315g	10oz
345g	11oz
375g	12oz (¾lb)
410g	13oz
440g	14oz
470g	15oz
500g	16oz (1lb)
750g	24oz (1½lb)
1kg	32oz (2lb)

LIQUID MEASURES

METRIC	IMPERIAL
30ml	1 fluid oz
60ml	2 fluid oz
100ml	3 fluid oz
125ml	4 fluid oz
150ml	5 fluid oz
190ml	6 fluid oz
250ml	8 fluid oz
300ml	10 fluid oz
500ml	16 fluid oz
600ml	20 fluid oz
1000ml (1 litre)	1¾ pints

LENGTH MEASURES

METRIC	IMPERIAL
3mm	⅛in
6mm	¼in
1cm	½in
2cm	¾in
2.5cm	1in
5cm	2in
6cm	2½in
8cm	3in
10cm	4in
13cm	5in
15cm	6in
18cm	7in
20cm	8in
22cm	9in
25cm	10in
28cm	11in
30cm	12in (1ft)

OVEN TEMPERATURES

The oven temperatures in this book are for conventional ovens;
if you have a fan-forced oven, decrease the temperature by 10-20 degrees.

	C CELSIUS	F FAHRENHEIT
Very slow	120	250
Slow	150	300
Moderately slow	160	325
Moderate	180	350
Moderately hot	200	400
Hot	220	425
Very hot	240	475

The imperial measurements used in these recipes are approximate only. Measurements for cake pans are approximate only. Using same-shaped cake pans of a similar size should not affect the outcome of your baking. We measure the inside top of the cake pan to determine sizes.

INDEX

This book is published in 2015 by Bounty Books, based on materials licensed to it by Bauer Media Books, Australia.
First published in 2012 by Bauer Media Books.

Bauer Media Books is a division of Bauer Media Pty Limited.

54 Park St, Sydney; GPO Box 4088, Sydney, NSW 2001, Australia

phone (+61) 2 9282 8618; fax (+61) 2 9126 3702

www.awwcookbooks.com.au

MEDIA GROUP

General manager Christine Whiston
Editor-in-chief Susan Tomnay
Creative director & designer Hieu Chi Nguyen
Senior editor Stephanie Kistner
Food director Pamela Clark
Senior food editor Rebecca Squadrito
Sales & rights director Brian Cearnes
Acting marketing manager Sonia Scali
Senior business analyst Rebecca Varela
Operations manager David Scotto
Production manager Victoria Jefferys

Photographer Steve Brown
Stylist Trish Heagerty
Photo chef Jerrie Lloyd

Published and Distributed in the United Kingdom by Octopus Publishing Group Ltd

An Hachette UK Company
www.hachette.co.uk

Carmelite House, 50 Victoria Embankment, London, EC4Y 0DZ
www.octopusbooks.co.uk

International foreign language rights,
Brian Cearnes, Bauer Media Books
bcearnes@bauer-media.com.au

All rights reserved. No part of this work may be reproduced or utilised in any form or by any means, electronic or mechanical, including photocopying, recording or by any information storage and retrieval system, without the prior written permission of the publisher.

A CIP catalogue record for this book is available from the British Library

ISBN: 978-0-7537-2988-5

© Bauer Media Pty Ltd 2012
ABN 18 053 273 546

Printed and bound in China

10 9 8 7 6 5 4 3 2 1